# THE UNDISCOVERED SELF

*with*

# SYMBOLS AND
# THE INTERPRETATION
# OF DREAMS

*from*

The Collected Works of C. G. Jung

*VOLUMES 10, 18*

BOLLINGEN SERIES XX

# THE UNDISCOVERED SELF

*with*

# SYMBOLS AND THE INTERPRETATION OF DREAMS

C. G. Jung

With a new foreword by
Sonu Shamdasani

*Translated and revised by R.F.C. Hull*

BOLLINGEN SERIES

PRINCETON UNIVERSITY PRESS
PRINCETON AND OXFORD

PUBLISHED BY PRINCETON UNIVERSITY PRESS, 41 WILLIAM STREET,
PRINCETON, NEW JERSEY 08540
PRESS.PRINCETON.EDU

*First Princeton/Bollingen Paperback printing, 1990*
*Paperback reissue, with a new foreword by Sonu Shamdasani, 2010*

LIBRARY OF CONGRESS CONTROL NUMBER: 2010934717
ISBN: 978-0-691-15051-2

Printed on acid-free paper. ∞

Printed in the United States of America

13

# TABLE OF CONTENTS

FOREWORD TO THE 2010 EDITION                        vii

The Undiscovered Self                                  1

Symbols and the Interpretation of Dreams             63

# FOREWORD TO THE 2010 EDITION

## READING JUNG AFTER *THE RED BOOK*

With the publication of *Liber Novus*—Jung's *Red Book*[1]—a new chapter opens in the reading of Jung's works. For the first time, one is in a position to grasp the constitution of Jung's work from 1914 onward, and to trace the intimate connections between his self-experimentation and his attempts to determine the typical features of this process through his work with his patients and translate his insights into a language acceptable to a medical and scientific public. Thus, reading *Liber Novus* brings with it the task of rereading Jung's *Collected Works*—much of which appears in a wholly new light.

In the winter of 1913, Jung embarked on a process of self-experimentation. He deliberately gave free rein to his fantasy thinking and carefully noted what ensued. He later called this process "active imagination." He wrote down these fantasies in the *Black Books*. These are not personal diaries, but rather the records of a self-experimentation. The dialogues that form these active imaginations can be regarded as a type of thinking in a dramatic form.

When World War I broke out, Jung considered that a number of his fantasies were precognitions of this event. This led him to compose the first draft of *Liber Novus*, which consisted of a transcription of the main fantasies from the *Black Books*, together with a layer of interpretive commentaries and lyrical elaboration. Here Jung attempted to derive general psychological principles from the fantasies, as well as to understand to what extent the events portrayed in the fantasies presented, in a symbolic form, developments that were to occur in the world.

Jung recopied the manuscript in an ornate Gothic script into a large red leather folio volume, which he illustrated with his own paintings.

---

[1] C. G. Jung, *The Red Book*, edited and introduced by Sonu Shamdasani and translated by Mark Kyburz, John Peck, and Sonu Shamdasani, Philemon Series (New York: W. W. Norton, 2009).

The overall theme of the book is how Jung regains his soul and overcomes the contemporary malaise of spiritual alienation. This is ultimately achieved by enabling the rebirth of a new image of God in his soul and developing a new worldview in the form of a psychological and theological cosmology.

Between 1916 and 1928, Jung published a number of works in which he attempted to translate some of the themes of *Liber Novus* into contemporary psychological language. In 1928, the sinologist Richard Wilhelm sent him a copy of the Taoist alchemical treatise *The Secret of the Golden Flower*, inviting him to write a commentary. Struck by the parallelism between the imagery of the text and some of his own mandalas, Jung finally decided to set aside his work on *Liber Novus* and not publish it. Instead he devoted himself to the cross-cultural study of the individuation process, focusing on medieval alchemy in particular, using parallels with his own material as a means to present the process in an indirect and allegorical form. Until now, this has presented formidable challenges for readers outside of Jung's inner circle.

## THE UNDISCOVERED SELF

In the aftermath of World War II, with the advent of the Cold War, the erection of the Berlin Wall, and the explosion of the hydrogen bomb, Jung found himself once again confronted with "An apocalyptic age filled with images of universal destruction,"[2] as he had been when he composed *Liber Novus* during World War I. Articulating there a direct linkage between what took place in the individual and in society at large, he argued that the only solution to the seemingly catastrophic developments in the world lay in the individual turning within and resolving the individual aspects of the collective conflict: "[T]he spirit of the depths wants this struggle [the War] to be understood as a conflict in every man's own nature."[3] In his personal confrontation, Jung's endeavor was one of resolving the conflicts that were reflected on the world stage within himself. In 1917, he wrote,

> This war has pitilessly revealed to civilized man that he is still a barbarian. . . . *But the psychology of the individual corresponds*

[2] See § 488, p. 94.
[3] *The Red Book*, p. 253.

*to the psychology of the nation.* What the nation does is done also by each individual, *and so long as the individual does it, the nation also does it.* Only the change in the attitude of the individual is the beginning of the change in the psychology of the nation.[4]

In the decades that followed, Jung's attempts to develop a psychology and psychotherapy of individuation were dedicated to this task. By the 1950s, modern history had shown that the predicament confronting the individual was even more extreme than in 1917. In 1956, Jung took up these themes once more, in a short work entitled in German *Present and Future* (retitled in English *The Undiscovered Self*). Articulating these themes within the contemporary historical context, he argued that only self-knowledge and religious experience could provide resistance to the totalitarian mass society. In this regard, the individual had been failed by modern science on one side, and by organized religion on the other. What was required was a psychology that facilitated self-knowledge by reconnecting individuals with their dreams and the symbols that spontaneously emerged from within—which was the theme of Jung's last written work, "Symbols and the Interpretation of Dreams," designed to convey his conceptions to a general public.

[4] *The Psychology of the Unconscious Processes, Collected Works* 7, p. 4.

# I

## THE UNDISCOVERED SELF

### (Present and Future)

# 1. THE PLIGHT OF THE INDIVIDUAL
## IN MODERN SOCIETY

488    What will the future bring? From time immemorial this question has occupied men's minds, though not always to the same degree. Historically, it is chiefly in times of physical, political, economic, and spiritual distress that men's eyes turn with anxious hope to the future, and when anticipations, utopias, and apocalyptic visions multiply. One thinks, for instance, of the chiliastic expectations of the Augustan age at the beginning of the Christian era, or of the spiritual changes in the West which accompanied the end of the first millennium. Today, as the end of the second millennium draws near, we are again living in an age filled with apocalyptic images of universal destruction. What is the significance of that split, symbolized by the "Iron Curtain," which divides humanity into two halves? What will become of our civilization, and of man himself, if the hydrogen bombs begin to go off, or if the spiritual and moral darkness of State absolutism should spread over Europe?

489    We have no reason to take this threat lightly. Everywhere in the West there are subversive minorities who, sheltered by our humanitarianism and our sense of justice, hold the incendiary torches ready, with nothing to stop the spread of their ideas except the critical reason of a single, fairly intelligent, mentally stable stratum of the population. One should not overestimate the thickness of this stratum. It varies from country to country in accordance with national temperament. Also, it is regionally dependent on public education and is subject to the influence of acutely disturbing factors of a political and economic nature. Taking plebiscites as a criterion, one could on an optimistic estimate put its upper limit at about forty per cent of the electorate. A rather more pessimistic view would not be unjustified either, since the gift of reason and critical reflection is not one of man's outstanding peculiarities, and even where it exists it proves to

3

be wavering and inconstant, the more so, as a rule, the bigger the political groups are. The mass crushes out the insight and reflection that are still possible with the individual, and this necessarily leads to doctrinaire and authoritarian tyranny if ever the constitutional State should succumb to a fit of weakness.

490    Rational argument can be conducted with some prospect of success only so long as the emotionality of a given situation does not exceed a certain critical degree. If the affective temperature rises above this level, the possibility of reason's having any effect ceases and its place is taken by slogans and chimerical wish-fantasies. That is to say, a sort of collective possession results which rapidly develops into a psychic epidemic. Under these conditions all those elements whose existence is merely tolerated as asocial under the rule of reason come to the top. Such individuals are by no means rare curiosities to be met with only in prisons and lunatic asylums. For every manifest case of insanity there are, in my estimation, at least ten latent cases who seldom get to the point of breaking out openly but whose views and behaviour, for all their appearance of normality, are influenced unconsciously by pathological and perverse factors. There are, of course, no medical statistics on the frequency of latent psychoses—for understandable reasons. But even if their number should amount to less than ten times that of the manifest psychoses and of manifest criminality, the relatively small percentage of the population figures they represent is more than compensated for by the peculiar dangerousness of these people. Their mental state is that of a collectively excited group ruled by affective judgments and wish-fantasies. In a milieu of this kind they are the adapted ones, and consequently they feel quite at home in it. They know from their own experience the language of these conditions, and they know how to handle them. Their chimerical ideas, sustained by fanatical resentment, appeal to the collective irrationality and find fruitful soil there; they express all those motives and resentments which lurk in more normal people under the cloak of reason and insight. They are, therefore, despite their small number in comparison with the population as a whole, dangerous as sources of infection precisely because the so-called normal person possesses only a limited degree of self-knowledge.

491    Most people confuse "self-knowledge" with knowledge of their conscious ego-personalities. Anyone who has any ego-consciousness at all takes it for granted that he knows himself. But the ego knows only its own contents, not the unconscious and its contents. People measure their self-knowledge by what the average person in their social environment knows of himself, but not by the real psychic facts which are for the most part hidden from them. In this respect the psyche behaves like the body, of whose physiological and anatomical structure the average person knows very little too. Although he lives in it and with it, most of it is totally unknown to the layman, and special scientific knowledge is needed to acquaint consciousness with what is known of the body, not to speak of all that is *not* known, which also exists.

492    What is commonly called "self-knowledge" is therefore a very limited knowledge, most of it dependent on social factors, of what goes on in the human psyche. Hence one is always coming up against the prejudice that such and such a thing does not happen "with us" or "in our family" or among our friends and acquaintances. On the other hand, one meets with equally illusory assumptions about the alleged presence of qualities which merely serve to cover up the true facts of the case.

493    In this broad belt of unconsciousness, which is immune to conscious criticism and control, we stand defenceless, open to all kinds of influences and psychic infections. As with all dangers, we can guard against the risk of psychic infection only when we know what is attacking us, and how, where and when the attack will come. Since self-knowledge is a matter of getting to know the individual facts, theories are of very little help. For the more a theory lays claim to universal validity, the less capable it is of doing justice to the individual facts. Any theory based on experience is necessarily *statistical;* it formulates an *ideal average* which abolishes all exceptions at either end of the scale and replaces them by an abstract mean. This mean is quite valid, though it need not necessarily occur in reality. Despite this it figures in the theory as an unassailable fundamental fact. The exceptions at either extreme, though equally factual, do not appear in the final result at all, since they cancel each other out. If, for instance, I determine the weight of each stone in a bed of pebbles and get an average weight of five ounces, this tells

me very little about the real nature of the pebbles. Anyone who thought, on the basis of these findings, that he could pick up a pebble of five ounces at the first try would be in for a serious disappointment. Indeed, it might well happen that however long he searched he would not find a single pebble weighing exactly five ounces.

494    The statistical method shows the facts in the light of the ideal average but does not give us a picture of their empirical reality. While reflecting an indisputable aspect of reality, it can falsify the actual truth in a most misleading way. This is particularly true of theories which are based on statistics. The distinctive thing about real facts, however, is their individuality. Not to put too fine a point on it, one could say that the real picture consists of nothing but exceptions to the rule, and that, in consequence, absolute reality has predominantly the character of *irregularity*.

495    These considerations must be borne in mind whenever there is talk of a theory serving as a guide to self-knowledge. There is and can be no self-knowledge based on theoretical assumptions, for the object of this knowledge is an individual—a relative exception and an irregular phenomenon. Hence it is not the universal and the regular that characterize the individual, but rather the unique. He is not to be understood as a recurrent unit but as something unique and singular which in the last analysis can be neither known nor compared with anything else. At the same time man, as member of a species, can and must be described as a statistical unit; otherwise nothing general could be said about him. For this purpose he has to be regarded as a comparative unit. This results in a universally valid anthropology or psychology, as the case may be, with an abstract picture of man as an average unit from which all individual features have been removed. But it is precisely these features which are of paramount importance for *understanding* man. If I want to understand an individual human being, I must lay aside all scientific knowledge of the average man and discard all theories in order to adopt a completely new and unprejudiced attitude. I can only approach the task of *understanding* with a free and open mind, whereas *knowledge* of man, or insight into human character, presupposes all sorts of knowledge about mankind in general.

496    Now whether it is a question of understanding a fellow human being or of self-knowledge, I must in both cases leave all theoretical assumptions behind me. Since scientific knowledge not only enjoys universal esteem but, in the eyes of modern man, counts as the only intellectual and spiritual authority, understanding the individual obliges me to commit the *lèse majesté,* so to speak, of turning a blind eye to scientific knowledge. This is a sacrifice not lightly made, for the scientific attitude cannot rid itself so easily of its sense of responsibility. And if the psychologist happens to be a doctor who wants not only to classify his patient scientifically but also to understand him as a human being, he is threatened with a conflict of duties between the two diametrically opposed and mutually exclusive attitudes of knowledge on the one hand and understanding on the other. This conflict cannot be solved by an either/or but only by a kind of two-way thinking: doing one thing while not losing sight of the other.

497    In view of the fact that, in principle, the positive advantages of *knowledge* work specifically to the disadvantage of *understanding,* the judgment resulting therefrom is likely to be something of a paradox. Judged scientifically, the individual is nothing but a unit which repeats itself *ad infinitum* and could just as well be designated with a letter of the alphabet. For understanding, on the other hand, it is just the unique individual human being who, when stripped of all those conformities and regularities so dear to the heart of the scientist, is the supreme and only real object of investigation. The doctor, above all, should be aware of this contradiction. On the one hand, he is equipped with the statistical truths of his scientific training, and on the other, he is faced with the task of treating a sick person who, especially in the case of psychic suffering, requires *individual understanding.* The more schematic the treatment is, the more resistances it—quite rightly—calls up in the patient, and the more the cure is jeopardized. The psychotherapist sees himself compelled, willy-nilly, to regard the individuality of a patient as an essential fact in the picture and to arrange his methods of treatment accordingly. Today, over the whole field of medicine, it is recognized that the task of the doctor consists in treating the sick person, not an abstract illness.

498    This illustration from the realm of medicine is only a special

7

instance of the problem of education and training in general. Scientific education is based in the main on statistical truths and abstract knowledge and therefore imparts an unrealistic, rational picture of the world, in which the individual, as a merely marginal phenomenon, plays no role. The individual, however, as an irrational datum, is the true and authentic carrier of reality, the *concrete* man as opposed to the unreal ideal or "normal" man to whom the scientific statements refer. What is more, most of the natural sciences try to represent the results of their investigations as though these had come into existence without man's intervention, in such a way that the collaboration of the psyche —an indispensable factor—remains invisible. (An exception to this is modern physics, which recognizes that the observed is not independent of the observer.) So, in this respect as well, science conveys a picture of the world from which a real human psyche appears to be excluded—the very antithesis of the "humanities."

499     Under the influence of scientific assumptions, not only the psyche but the individual man and, indeed, all individual events whatsoever suffer a levelling down and a process of blurring that distorts the picture of reality into a conceptual average. We ought not to underestimate the psychological effect of the statistical world-picture: it thrusts aside the individual in favour of anonymous units that pile up into mass formations. Instead of the concrete individual, you have the names of organizations and, at the highest point, the abstract idea of the State as the principle of political reality. The moral responsibility of the individual is then inevitably replaced by the policy of the State (*raison d'état*). Instead of moral and mental differentiation of the individual, you have public welfare and the raising of the living standard. The goal and meaning of individual life (which is the only *real* life) no longer lie in individual development but in the policy of the State, which is thrust upon the individual from outside and consists in the execution of an abstract idea which ultimately tends to attract all life to itself. The individual is increasingly deprived of the moral decision as to how he should live his own life, and instead is ruled, fed, clothed, and educated as a social unit, accommodated in the appropriate housing unit, and amused in accordance with the standards that give pleasure and satisfaction to the masses. The rulers, in their turn, are just as much social units as the ruled, and are distin-

8

guished only by the fact that they are specialized mouthpieces of the State doctrine. They do not need to be personalities capable of judgment, but thoroughgoing specialists who are unusable outside their line of business. State policy decides what shall be taught and studied.

500     The seemingly omnipotent State doctrine is for its part manipulated in the name of State policy by those occupying the highest positions in the government, where all the power is concentrated. Whoever, by election or caprice, gets into one of these positions is subject to no higher authority; he is the State policy itself and within the limits of the situation can proceed at his own discretion. With Louis XIV he can say, "L'état c'est moi." He is thus the only individual or, at any rate, one of the few individuals who could make use of their individuality if only they knew how to differentiate themselves from the State doctrine. They are more likely, however, to be the slaves of their own fictions. Such one-sidedness is always compensated psychologically by unconscious subversive tendencies. Slavery and rebellion are inseparable correlates. Hence, rivalry for power and exaggerated distrust pervade the entire organism from top to bottom. Furthermore, in order to compensate for its chaotic formlessness, a mass always produces a "Leader," who infallibly becomes the victim of his own inflated ego-consciousness, as numerous examples in history show.

501     This development becomes logically unavoidable the moment the individual combines with the mass and thus renders himself obsolete. Apart from the agglomeration of huge masses in which the individual disappears anyway, one of the chief factors responsible for psychological mass-mindedness is scientific rationalism, which robs the individual of his foundations and his dignity. As a social unit he has lost his individuality and become a mere abstract number in the bureau of statistics. He can only play the role of an interchangeable unit of infinitesimal importance. Looked at rationally and from outside, that is exactly what he is, and from this point of view it seems positively absurd to go on talking about the value or meaning of the individual. Indeed, one can hardly imagine how one ever came to endow individual human life with so much dignity when the truth to the contrary is as plain as the palm of your hand.

502     Seen from this standpoint, the individual really is of dimin-

ishing importance and anyone who wished to dispute this would soon find himself at a loss for arguments. The fact that the individual feels himself or the members of his family or the esteemed friends in his circle to be important merely underlines the slightly comic subjectivity of his feeling. For what are the few compared with ten thousand or a hundred thousand, let alone a million? This recalls the argument of a thoughtful friend with whom I once got caught up in a huge crowd of people. Suddenly he exclaimed, "Here you have the most convincing reason for not believing in immortality: all *that lot* wants to be immortal!"

503    The bigger the crowd the more negligible the individual becomes. But if the individual, overwhelmed by the sense of his own puniness and impotence, should feel that his life has lost its meaning—which, after all, is not identical with public welfare and higher standards of living—then he is already on the road to State slavery and, without knowing or wanting it, has become its proselyte. The man who looks only outside and quails before the big battalions has nothing with which to combat the evidence of his senses and his reason. But that is just what is happening today: we are all fascinated and overawed by statistical truths and large numbers and are daily apprised of the nullity and futility of the individual personality, since it is not represented and personified by any mass organization. Conversely, those personages who strut about on the world stage and whose voices are heard far and wide seem, to the uncritical public, to be borne along on some mass movement or on the tide of public opinion and for this reason are either applauded or execrated. Since mass suggestion plays the predominant role here, it remains a moot point whether their message is their own, for which they are personally responsible, or whether they merely function as a megaphone for collective opinion.

504    Under these circumstances it is small wonder that individual judgment grows increasingly uncertain of itself and that responsibility is collectivized as much as possible, i.e., is shuffled off by the individual and delegated to a corporate body. In this way the individual becomes more and more a function of society, which in its turn usurps the function of the real life carrier, whereas, in actual fact, society is nothing more than an abstract idea like the State. Both are hypostatized, that is, have become

10

autonomous. The State in particular is turned into a quasi-animate personality from whom everything is expected. In reality it is only a camouflage for those individuals who know how to manipulate it. Thus the constitutional State drifts into the situation of a primitive form of society—the communism of a primitive tribe where everybody is subject to the autocratic rule of a chief or an oligarchy.

## 2. RELIGION AS THE COUNTERBALANCE TO MASS-MINDEDNESS

505    In order to free the fiction of the sovereign State—in other words, the whims of the chieftains who manipulate it—from every wholesome restriction, all socio-political movements tending in this direction invariably try to cut the ground from under *religion*. For, in order to turn the individual into a function of the State, his dependence on anything else must be taken from him. Religion means dependence on and submission to the irrational facts of experience. These do not refer directly to social and physical conditions; they concern far more the individual's psychic attitude.

506    But it is possible to have an attitude to the external conditions of life only when there is a point of reference outside them. Religion gives, or claims to give, such a standpoint, thereby enabling the individual to exercise his judgment and his power of decision. It builds up a reserve, as it were, against the obvious and inevitable force of circumstances to which everyone is exposed who lives only in the outer world and has no other ground under his feet except the pavement. If statistical reality is the only one, then that is the sole authority. There is then only *one* condition, and since no contrary condition exists, judgment and decision are not only superfluous but impossible. Then the individual is bound to be a function of statistics and hence a function of the State or whatever the abstract principle of order may be called.

507    Religion, however, teaches another authority opposed to that of the "world." The doctrine of the individual's dependence on God makes just as high a claim upon him as the world does. It may even happen that the absoluteness of this claim estranges him from the world in the same way as he is estranged from himself when he succumbs to the collective mentality. He can forfeit his judgment and power of decision in the former

case (for the sake of religious doctrine) quite as much as in the latter. This is the goal which religion openly aspires to unless it compromises with the State. When it does so, I prefer to call it not "religion" but a "creed." A creed gives expression to a definite collective belief, whereas the word *religion* expresses a subjective relationship to certain metaphysical, extramundane factors. A creed is a confession of faith intended chiefly for the world at large and is thus an intramundane affair, while the meaning and purpose of religion lie in the relationship of the individual to God (Christianity, Judaism, Islam) or to the path of salvation and liberation (Buddhism). From this basic fact all ethics is derived, which without the individual's responsibility before God can be called nothing more than conventional morality.

508    Since they are compromises with mundane reality, the creeds have accordingly seen themselves obliged to undertake a progressive codification of their views, doctrines, and customs, and in so doing have externalized themselves to such an extent that the authentic religious element in them—the living relationship to and direct confrontation with their extramundane point of reference—has been thrust into the background. The denominational standpoint measures the worth and importance of the subjective religious relationship by the yardstick of traditional doctrine, and where this is not so frequent, as in Protestantism, one immediately hears talk of pietism, sectarianism, eccentricity, and so forth, as soon as anyone claims to be guided by God's will. A creed coincides with the established Church or, at any rate, forms a public institution whose members include not only true believers but vast numbers of people who can only be described as "indifferent" in matters of religion and who belong to it simply by force of habit. Here the difference between a creed and a religion becomes palpable.

509    To be the adherent of a creed, therefore, is not always a religious matter but more often a social one and, as such, it does nothing to give the individual any foundation. For this he has to depend exclusively on his relation to an authority which is not of this world. The criterion here is not lip service to a creed but the psychological fact that the life of the individual is not determined solely by the ego and its opinions or by social factors, but quite as much, if not more, by a transcendent author-

ity. It is not ethical principles, however lofty, or creeds, however orthodox, that lay the foundations for the freedom and autonomy of the individual, but simply and solely the empirical awareness, the incontrovertible experience of an intensely personal, reciprocal relationship between man and an extramundane authority which acts as a counterpoise to the "world" and its "reason."

510     This formulation will not please either the mass man or the collective believer. For the former the policy of the State is the supreme principle of thought and action. Indeed, this was the purpose for which he was enlightened, and accordingly the mass man grants the individual a right to exist only in so far as he is a function of the State. The believer, on the other hand, while admitting that the State has a moral and factual claim on him, confesses to the belief that not only man but the State that rules him is subject to the overlordship of "God," and that, in case of doubt, the supreme decision will be made by God and not by the State. Since I do not presume to any metaphysical judgments, I must leave it an open question whether the "world," i.e., the phenomenal world of man, and hence nature in general, is the "opposite" of God or not. I can only point to the fact that the psychological opposition between these two realms of experience is not only vouched for in the New Testament but is still exemplified very plainly today in the negative attitude of the dictator States to religion and of the Church to atheism and materialism.

511     Just as man, as a social being, cannot in the long run exist without a tie to the community, so the individual will never find the real justification for his existence and his own spiritual and moral autonomy anywhere except in an extramundane principle capable of relativizing the overpowering influence of external factors. The individual who is not anchored in God can offer no resistance on his own resources to the physical and moral blandishments of the world. For this he needs the evidence of inner, transcendent experience which alone can protect him from the otherwise inevitable submersion in the mass. Merely intellectual or even moral insight into the stultification and moral irresponsibility of the mass man is a negative recognition only and amounts to not much more than a wavering on the road to the atomization of the individual. It lacks the driv-

ing force of religious conviction, since it is merely rational. The dictator State has one great advantage over bourgeois reason: along with the individual it swallows up his religious forces. The State takes the place of God; that is why, seen from this angle, the socialist dictatorships are religions and State slavery is a form of worship. But the religious function cannot be dislocated and falsified in this way without giving rise to secret doubts, which are immediately repressed so as to avoid conflict with the prevailing trend towards mass-mindedness. The result, as always in such cases, is overcompensation in the form of *fanaticism,* which in its turn is used as a weapon for stamping out the least flicker of opposition. Free opinion is stifled and moral decision ruthlessly suppressed, on the plea that the end justifies the means, even the vilest. The policy of the State is exalted to a creed, the leader or party boss becomes a demigod beyond good and evil, and his votaries are honoured as heroes, martyrs, apostles, missionaries. There is only *one* truth and beside it no other. It is sacrosanct and above criticism. Anyone who thinks differently is a heretic, who, as we know from history, is threatened with all manner of unpleasant things. Only the party boss, who holds the political power in his hands, can interpret the State doctrine authentically, and he does so just as suits him.

512    When, through mass rule, the individual becomes social unit No. so-and-so and the State is elevated to the supreme principle, it is only to be expected that the religious function too will be sucked into the maelstrom. Religion, as the careful observation and taking account of certain invisible and uncontrollable factors, is an *instinctive* attitude peculiar to man, and its manifestations can be followed all through human history. Its evident purpose is to maintain the psychic balance, for the natural man has an equally natural "knowledge" of the fact that his conscious functions may at any time be thwarted by uncontrollable happenings coming from inside as well as from outside. For this reason he has always taken care that any difficult decision likely to have consequences for himself and others shall be rendered safe by suitable measures of a religious nature. Offerings are made to the invisible powers, formidable blessings are pronounced, and all kinds of solemn rites are performed. Everywhere and at all times there have been *rites d'entrée et de sortie*

whose efficacy is impugned as magic and superstition by rationalists incapable of psychological insight. But magic has above all a psychological effect whose importance should not be underestimated. The performance of a "magical" action gives the person concerned a feeling of security which is absolutely essential for carrying out a decision, because a decision is inevitably somewhat one-sided and is therefore rightly felt to be a risk. Even a dictator thinks it necessary not only to accompany his acts of State with threats but to stage them with all manner of solemnities. Brass bands, flags, banners, parades, and monster demonstrations are no different in principle from ecclesiastical processions, cannonades, and fireworks to scare off demons. Only, the suggestive parade of State power engenders a collective feeling of security which, unlike religious demonstrations, gives the individual no protection against his inner demonism. Hence he will cling all the more to the power of the State, i.e., to the mass, thus delivering himself up to it psychically as well as morally and putting the finishing touch to his social depotentiation. The State, like the Church, demands enthusiasm, self-sacrifice, and love, and if religion requires or presupposes the "fear of God," then the dictator State takes good care to provide the necessary terror.

513    When the rationalist directs the main force of his attack against the miraculous effect of the rite as asserted by tradition, he has in reality completely missed the mark. The essential point, the *psychological* effect, is overlooked, although both parties make use of it for directly opposite purposes. A similar situation prevails with regard to their respective conceptions of the goal. The goals of religion—deliverance from evil, reconciliation with God, rewards in the hereafter, and so on—turn into worldly promises about freedom from care for one's daily bread, the just distribution of material goods, universal prosperity in the future, and shorter working hours. That the fulfilment of these promises is as far off as Paradise only furnishes yet another analogy and underlines the fact that the masses have been converted from an extramundane goal to a purely worldly belief, which is extolled with exactly the same religious fervour and exclusiveness that the creeds display in the other direction.

514    In order not to repeat myself unnecessarily, I shall not enumerate all the parallels between worldly and otherworldly be-

liefs, but shall content myself with emphasizing the fact that a natural function which has existed from the beginning, like the religious function, cannot be disposed of with rationalistic and so-called enlightened criticism. You can, of course, represent the doctrinal contents of the creeds as impossible and subject them to ridicule, but such methods miss the point and do not affect the religious function which forms the basis of the creeds. Religion, in the sense of conscientious regard for the irrational factors of the psyche and individual fate, reappears—evilly distorted—in the deification of the State and the dictator: *Naturam expellas furca tamen usque recurret* (You can throw out Nature with a pitchfork, but she'll always turn up again). The leaders and dictators, having weighed up the situation correctly, are therefore doing their best to gloss over the all too obvious parallel with the deification of Caesar and to hide their real power behind the fiction of the State, though this, of course, alters nothing.[1]

515     As I have already pointed out, the dictator State, besides robbing the individual of his rights, has also cut the ground from under his feet psychically by depriving him of the metaphysical foundations of his existence. The ethical decision of the individual human being no longer counts—what alone matters is the blind movement of the masses, and the *lie* thus becomes the operative principle of political action. The State has drawn the logical conclusions from this, as the existence of many millions of State slaves completely deprived of all rights mutely testifies.

516     Both the dictator State and denominational religion lay quite particular emphasis on the idea of *community*. This is the basic ideal of "communism," and it is thrust down the throats of the people so much that it has the exact opposite of the desired effect: it inspires divisive mistrust. The Church, which is no less emphatic, appears on its side as a communal ideal, and where the Church is notoriously weak, as in Protestantism, the hope of or belief in a "communal experience" makes up for the painful lack of cohesion. As can easily be seen, "community" is an indispensable aid in the organization of masses and is therefore a two-edged weapon. Just as the addition of however many

1 Since this essay was written, in the spring of 1956, there has been a noticeable reaction in the U.S.S.R. to this objectionable state of affairs.

zeros will never make a unit, so the value of a community depends on the spiritual and moral stature of the individuals composing it. For this reason one cannot expect from the community any effect that would outweigh the suggestive influence of the environment—that is, a real and fundamental change in individuals, whether for good or for bad. Such changes can come only from the personal encounter between man and man, but not from communistic or Christian baptisms *en masse,* which do not touch the inner man. How superficial the effect of communal propaganda actually is can be seen from recent events in Eastern Europe.[2] The communal ideal reckons without its host, overlooking the individual human being, who in the end will assert his claims.

2 Added in January 1957.

## 3. THE POSITION OF THE WEST ON
## THE QUESTION OF RELIGION

517      Confronting this development in the twentieth century of
our Christian era, the Western world stands with its heritage of
Roman law, the treasures of Judaeo-Christian ethics grounded
on metaphysics, and its ideal of the inalienable rights of man.
Anxiously it asks itself the question: How can this development
be brought to a standstill or put into reverse? It is useless to
pillory the socialist dictatorship as utopian and to condemn its
economic principles as unreasonable, because, in the first place,
the criticizing West has only itself to talk to, its arguments being heard only on this side of the Iron Curtain, and, in the second place, any economic principles you like can be put into
practice so long as you are prepared to accept the sacrifices they
entail. You can carry through any social and economic reforms
you please if, like Stalin, you let three million peasants starve to
death and have a few million unpaid labourers at your disposal.
A State of this kind has no social or economic crises to fear. So
long as its power is intact—that is to say, so long as there is a
well-disciplined and well-fed police army in the offing—it can
maintain its existence for an indefinitely long period and can
go on increasing its power to an indefinite extent. Thanks to its
excess birth-rate, it can multiply the number of its unpaid
workers almost at will in order to compete with its rivals, re-
gardless of the world market, which is to a large measure dependent on wages. A real danger can come to it only from outside, through the threat of military attack. But this risk grows
less every year, firstly because the war potential of the dictator
States is steadily increasing, and secondly because the West cannot afford to arouse latent Russian or Chinese nationalism and
chauvinism by an attack which would have exactly the opposite
effect to the one intended.

518      So far as one can see, only one possibility remains, and that

is a break-down of power from within, which must, however, be left to follow its own inner development. Any support from outside at present would have little effect, in view of the existing security measures and the danger of nationalistic reactions. The absolute State has an army of fanatical missionaries to do its bidding in matters of foreign policy, and these in their turn can count on a fifth column who are guaranteed asylum under the laws and constitutions of the Western States. In addition the communes of believers, very strong in places, considerably weaken Western governments' powers of decision, whereas the West has no opportunity to exert a similar influence on the other side, though we are probably not wrong in surmising that there is a certain amount of opposition among the masses in the East. There are always upright and truth-loving people to whom lying and tyranny are hateful, but one cannot judge whether they exert any decisive influence on the masses under the police régimes.[1]

519    In view of this uncomfortable situation the question is heard again and again in the West: What can we do to counter this threat from the East? Even though the West has considerable industrial power and a sizable defence potential at its command, we cannot rest content with this, for we know that even the biggest armaments and the heaviest industry coupled with a relatively high living standard are not enough to check the psychic infection spread by religious fanaticism.

520    The West has unfortunately not yet woken up to the fact that our appeal to idealism and reason and other desirable virtues, delivered with so much enthusiasm, is mere bombination in the void. It is a puff of wind swept away in the storm of religious faith, however twisted this faith may appear to us. We are faced, not with a situation that can be overcome by rational or moral arguments, but with an unleashing of emotional forces and ideas engendered by the spirit of the times; and these, as we know from experience, are not much influenced by rational reflection and still less by moral exhortation. It has been correctly realized in many quarters that the alexipharmic, the antidote, should in this case be an equally potent faith of a different and non-materialistic kind, and that the religious attitude

[1] Recent events in Poland and Hungary have shown that this opposition is more considerable than could have been foreseen [1956].

grounded upon it would be the only effective defence against the danger of psychic infection. Unhappily, the little word "should," which never fails to appear in this connection, points to a certain weakness, if not the absence, of this desideratum. Not only does the West lack a uniform faith that could block the progress of a fanatical ideology, but, as the father of Marxist philosophy, it makes use of exactly the same intellectual assumptions, the same arguments and aims. Although the Churches in the West enjoy full freedom, they are not less full or empty than in the East. Yet they exercise no noticeable influence on the broad course of politics. The disadvantage of a creed as a public institution is that it serves two masters: on the one hand, it derives its existence from the relationship of man to God, and on the other hand, it owes a duty to the State, i.e., to the world, in which connection it can appeal to the saying "Render unto Caesar . . ." and various other admonitions in the New Testament.

521   In early times and until comparatively recently there was, therefore, talk of "powers ordained by God" (Romans 13 : 1). Today this conception is antiquated. The Churches stand for traditional and collective convictions which in the case of many of their adherents are no longer based on their own inner experience but on *unreflecting belief,* which is notoriously apt to disappear as soon as one begins thinking about it. The content of belief then comes into collision with knowledge, and it often turns out that the irrationality of the former is no match for the ratiocinations of the latter. Belief is no adequate substitute for inner experience, and where this is absent even a strong faith which came miraculously as a gift of grace may depart equally miraculously. People call faith the true religious experience, but they do not stop to consider that actually it is a secondary phenomenon arising from the fact that something happened to us in the first place which instilled πίστις into us— that is, trust and loyalty. This experience has a definite content that can be interpreted in terms of one or other of the denominational creeds. But the more this is so, the more the possibilities of these conflicts with knowledge mount up, which in themselves are quite pointless. That is to say, the standpoint of the creeds is archaic; they are full of impressive mythological symbolism which, if taken literally, comes into insufferable con-

21

flict with knowledge. But if, for instance, the statement that Christ rose from the dead is to be understood not literally but symbolically, then it is capable of various interpretations that do not conflict with knowledge and do not impair the meaning of the statement. The objection that understanding it symbolically puts an end to the Christian's hope of immortality is invalid, because long before the coming of Christianity mankind believed in a life after death and therefore had no need of the Easter event as a guarantee of immortality. The danger that a mythology understood too literally, and as taught by the Church, will suddenly be repudiated lock, stock and barrel is today greater than ever. Is it not time that the Christian mythology, instead of being wiped out, was understood symbolically for once?

522    It is still too early to say what might be the consequences of a general recognition of the fatal parallelism between the State religion of the Marxists and the State religion of the Church. The absolutist claim of a *Civitas Dei* that is represented by man bears an unfortunate resemblance to the "divinity" of the State, and the moral conclusion drawn by Ignatius Loyola from the authority of the Church ("the end sanctifies the means") anticipates the lie as a political instrument in an exceedingly dangerous way. Both demand unqualified submission to faith and thus curtail man's freedom, the one his freedom before God and the other his freedom before the State, thereby digging the grave for the individual. The fragile existence of this—so far as we know—unique carrier of life is threatened on both sides, despite their respective promises of spiritual and material idylls to come—and how many of us can in the long run fight against the proverbial wisdom of "a bird in the hand is worth two in the bush"? Besides which, the West cherishes the same "scientific" and rationalistic *Weltanschauung* with its statistical levelling-down tendency and materialistic aims as the State religion of the Eastern bloc, as I have explained above.

523    What, then, has the West, with its political and denominational schisms, to offer to modern man in his need? Nothing, unfortunately, except a variety of paths all leading to one goal which is practically indistinguishable from the Marxist ideal. It requires no special effort of understanding to see where the Communist ideology gets the certainty of its belief that time

is on its side, and that the world is ripe for conversion. The facts speak a language that is all too plain in this respect. It will not help us in the West to shut our eyes to this and not recognize our fatal vulnerability. Anyone who has once learned to submit absolutely to a collective belief and to renounce his eternal right to freedom and the equally eternal duty of individual responsibility will persist in this attitude, and will be able to march with the same credulity and the same lack of criticism in the reverse direction, if another and manifestly "better" belief is foisted upon his alleged idealism. What happened not so long ago to a civilized European nation? We accuse the Germans of having forgotten it all again already, but the truth is that we don't know for certain whether something similar might not happen elsewhere. It would not be surprising if it did and if another civilized nation succumbed to the infection of a uniform and one-sided idea. We permit ourselves the question: which countries have the biggest Communist parties? America, which—*O quae mutatio rerum!*—forms the real political backbone of Western Europe, seems to be immune because of the outspoken counterposition she has adopted, but in point of fact she is perhaps even more vulnerable than Europe, since her educational system is the most influenced by the scientific *Weltanschauung* with its statistical truths, and her mixed population finds it difficult to strike roots in a soil that is practically without history. The historical and humanistic type of education so sorely needed in such circumstances leads, on the contrary, a Cinderella existence. Though Europe possesses this latter requirement, she uses it to her own undoing in the form of nationalistic egoisms and paralysing scepticism. Common to both is the materialistic and collectivist goal, and both lack the very thing that expresses and grips the whole man, namely, an idea which puts the individual human being in the centre as the measure of all things.

524    This idea alone is enough to arouse the most violent doubts and resistances on all sides, and one could almost go so far as to assert that the valuelessness of the individual in comparison with large numbers is the one belief that meets with universal and unanimous assent. To be sure, we all say that this is the century of the common man, that he is the lord of the earth, the air, and the water, and that on his decision hangs the historical

fate of the nations. This proud picture of human grandeur is unfortunately an illusion and is counterbalanced by a reality that is very different. In this reality man is the slave and victim of the machines that have conquered space and time for him; he is intimidated and endangered by the might of the military technology which is supposed to safeguard his physical existence; his spiritual and moral freedom, though guaranteed within limits in one half of his world, is threatened with chaotic disorientation, and in the other half is abolished altogether. Finally, to add comedy to tragedy, this lord of the elements, this universal arbiter, hugs to his bosom notions which stamp his dignity as worthless and turn his autonomy into an absurdity. All his achievements and possessions do not make him bigger; on the contrary, they diminish him, as the fate of the factory-worker under the rule of a "just" distribution of goods clearly demonstrates. He pays for his share of the factory with the loss of personal property, he exchanges his freedom of movement for the doubtful pleasure of being tied to his place of employment, he forfeits all means of improving his position if he jibs against being ground down by exhausting piece-work, and if he shows any signs of intelligence, political precepts are thrust down his throat—with a bit of technical knowledge thrown in, if he is lucky. However, a roof over one's head and a daily feed for the useful animal are not to be sneezed at when the bare necessities of life may be cut off from one day to the next.

## 4. THE INDIVIDUAL'S UNDERSTANDING
## OF HIMSELF

525   It is astounding that man, the instigator, inventor and vehicle of all these developments, the originator of all judgments and decisions and the planner of the future, must make himself such a *quantité négligeable*. The contradiction, the paradoxical evaluation of humanity by man himself, is in truth a matter for wonder, and one can only explain it as springing from an extraordinary uncertainty of judgment—in other words, man is an enigma to himself. This is understandable, seeing that he lacks the means of comparison necessary for self-knowledge. He knows how to distinguish himself from the other animals in point of anatomy and physiology, but as a conscious, reflecting being, gifted with speech, he lacks all criteria for self-judgment. He is on this planet a unique phenomenon which he cannot compare with anything else. The possibility of comparison and hence of self-knowledge would arise only if he could establish relations with quasi-human mammals inhabiting other stars.

526   Until then man must continue to resemble a hermit who knows that in respect of comparative anatomy he has affinities with the anthropoids but, to judge by appearances, is extraordinarily different from his cousins in respect of his psyche. It is just in this most important characteristic of his species that he cannot know himself and therefore remains a mystery to himself. The differing degrees of self-knowledge within his own species are of little significance compared with the possibilities which would be opened out by an encounter with a creature of similar structure but different origin. Our psyche, which is primarily responsible for all the historical changes wrought by the hand of man on the face of this planet, remains an insoluble puzzle and an incomprehensible wonder, an object of abiding perplexity—a feature it shares with all Nature's secrets.

In regard to the latter we still have hope of making more discoveries and finding answers to the most difficult questions. But in regard to the psyche and psychology there seems to be a curious hesitancy. Not only is it the youngest of the empirical sciences, but it has great difficulty in getting anywhere near its proper object.

527     In the same way that our picture of the world had to be freed by Copernicus from the prejudice of geocentricity, the most strenuous efforts of a well-nigh revolutionary nature were needed to free psychology, first from the spell of mythological ideas, and then from the prejudice that the psyche is, on the one hand, a mere epiphenomenon of a biochemical process in the brain and, on the other hand, a purely personal matter. The connection with the brain does not in itself prove that the psyche is an epiphenomenon, a secondary function causally dependent on biochemical processes in the physical substrate. Nevertheless, we know only too well how much the psychic function can be disturbed by verifiable processes in the brain, and this fact is so impressive that the subsidiary nature of the psyche seems an almost unavoidable inference. The phenomena of parapsychology, however, warn us to be careful, for they point to a relativization of space and time through psychic factors which casts doubt on our naïve and overhasty explanation in terms of psychophysical parallelism. For the sake of this explanation people deny the findings of parapsychology outright, either for philosophical reasons or from intellectual laziness. This can hardly be considered a scientifically responsible attitude, even though it is a popular way out of a quite extraordinary intellectual difficulty. To assess the psychic phenomenon, we have to take account of all the other phenomena that go with it, and accordingly we can no longer practise any psychology that ignores the existence of the unconscious or of parapsychology.

528     The structure and physiology of the brain furnish no explanation of the psychic process. The psyche has a peculiar nature which cannot be reduced to anything else. Like physiology, it presents a relatively self-contained field of experience, to which we must attribute a quite special importance because it includes one of the two indispensable conditions for existence as such, namely, the phenomenon of consciousness. Without conscious-

ness there would, practically speaking, be no world, for the world exists for us only in so far as it is consciously reflected by a psyche. *Consciousness is a precondition of being.* Thus the psyche is endowed with the dignity of a cosmic principle, which philosophically and in fact gives it a position co-equal with the principle of physical being. The carrier of this consciousness is the individual, who does not produce the psyche of his own volition but is, on the contrary, preformed by it and nourished by the gradual awakening of consciousness during childhood. If therefore the psyche is of overriding empirical importance, so also is the individual, who is the only immediate manifestation of the psyche.

529    This fact must be expressly emphasized for two reasons. Firstly, the individual psyche, just because of its individuality, is an exception to the statistical rule and is therefore robbed of one of its main characteristics when subjected to the levelling influence of statistical evaluation. Secondly, the Churches grant it validity only in so far as it acknowledges their dogmas—in other words, when it submits to a collective category. In both cases the will to individuality is regarded as egotistic obstinacy. Science devalues this as subjectivism, and the Churches condemn it morally as heresy and spiritual pride. As to the latter charge, it should not be forgotten that, unlike other religions, Christianity holds up before us a symbol whose content is the individual way of life of a man, the Son of Man, and that it even regards this individuation process as the incarnation and revelation of God himself. Hence the development of man into a self acquires a significance whose full implications have hardly begun to be appreciated, because too much attention to externals blocks the way to immediate inner experience. Were not the autonomy of the individual the secret longing of many people it would scarcely be able to survive the collective suppression either morally or spiritually.

530    All these obstacles make it more difficult to arrive at a correct appreciation of the human psyche, but they count for very little beside one other remarkable fact that deserves mentioning. This is the common psychiatric experience that the devaluation of the psyche and other resistances to psychological enlightenment are based in large measure on fear—on panic fear of the discoveries that might be made in the realm of the uncon-

scious. These fears are found not only among persons who are frightened by the picture Freud painted of the unconscious; they also troubled the originator of psychoanalysis himself, who confessed to me that it was necessary to make a dogma of his sexual theory because this was the sole bulwark of reason against a possible "eruption of the black flood of occultism." In these words Freud was expressing his conviction that the unconscious still harboured many things that might lend themselves to "occult" interpretation, as is in fact the case. These "archaic vestiges," or archetypal forms grounded on the instincts and giving expression to them, have a numinous quality that sometimes arouses fear. They are ineradicable, for they represent the ultimate foundations of the psyche itself. They cannot be grasped intellectually, and when one has destroyed one manifestation of them, they reappear in altered form. It is this fear of the unconscious psyche which not only impedes self-knowledge but is the gravest obstacle to a wider understanding and knowledge of psychology. Often the fear is so great that one dares not admit it even to oneself. This is a question which every religious person should consider very seriously; he might get an illuminating answer.

531    A scientifically oriented psychology is bound to proceed abstractly; that is, it removes itself just sufficiently far from its object not to lose sight of it altogether. That is why the findings of laboratory psychology are, for all practical purposes, often so remarkably unenlightening and devoid of interest. The more the individual object dominates the field of vision, the more practical, detailed, and alive will be the knowledge derived from it. This means that the objects of investigation, too, become more and more complicated and that the uncertainty of the individual factors grows in proportion to their number, thus increasing the possibility of error. Understandably enough, academic psychology is scared of this risk and prefers to avoid complex situations by asking ever simpler questions, which it can do with impunity. It has full freedom in the choice of questions it will put to Nature.

532    Medical psychology, on the other hand, is very far from being in this more or less enviable position. Here the object puts the question and not the experimenter. The analyst is confronted with facts which are not of his choosing and which he probably

never *would* choose if he were a free agent. It is the sickness or the patient himself that puts the crucial questions—in other words, Nature experiments with the doctor in expecting an answer from him. The uniqueness of the individual and of his situation stares the analyst in the face and demands an answer. His duty as a physician forces him to cope with a situation swarming with uncertainty factors. At first he will apply principles based on general experience, but he will soon realize that principles of this kind do not adequately express the facts and fail to meet the nature of the case. The deeper his understanding penetrates, the more the general principles lose their meaning. But these principles are the foundation of objective knowledge and the yardstick by which it is measured. With the growth of what both patient and doctor feel to be "understanding," the situation becomes increasingly subjectivized. What was an advantage to begin with threatens to turn into a dangerous disadvantage. Subjectivation (in technical terms, transference and countertransference) creates isolation from the environment, a social limitation which neither party wishes for but which invariably sets in when understanding predominates and is no longer balanced by knowledge. As understanding deepens, the further removed it becomes from knowledge. An ideal understanding would ultimately result in each party's unthinkingly going along with the other's experience—a state of uncritical passivity coupled with the most complete subjectivity and lack of social responsibility. Understanding carried to such lengths is in any case impossible, for it would require the virtual identification of two different individuals. Sooner or later the relationship reaches a point where one partner feels he is being forced to sacrifice his own individuality so that it may be assimilated by that of the other. This inevitable consequence breaks the understanding, for understanding also presupposes the integral preservation of the individuality of both partners. It is therefore advisable to carry understanding only to the point where the balance between understanding and knowledge is reached, for understanding at all costs is injurious to both partners.

533    This problem arises whenever complex, individual situations have to be known and understood. It is the specific task of the medical psychologist to provide just this knowledge and

understanding. It would also be the task of the "director of conscience" zealous in the cure of souls, were it not that his office inevitably obliges him to apply the yardstick of his denominational bias at the critical moment. As a result, the individual's right to exist as such is cut short by a collective prejudice and often curtailed in the most sensitive area. The only time this does not happen is when the dogmatic symbol, for instance the model life of Christ, is understood concretely and felt by the individual to be adequate. How far this is the case today I would prefer to leave to the judgment of others. At all events, the analyst very often has to treat patients to whom denominational limitations mean little or nothing. His profession therefore compels him to have as few preconceptions as possible. Similarly, while respecting metaphysical (i.e., non-verifiable) convictions and assertions, he will take care not to credit them with universal validity. This caution is called for because the individual traits of the patient's personality ought not to be twisted out of shape by arbitrary interventions from outside. The analyst must leave this to environmental influences, to the patient's own inner development, and—in the widest sense—to fate with its wise or unwise decrees.

534    Many people will perhaps find this heightened caution exaggerated. In view of the fact, however, that there is in any case such a multitude of reciprocal influences at work in the dialectical process between two individuals, even if it is conducted with the most tactful reserve, the responsible analyst will refrain from adding unnecessarily to the collective factors to which his patient has already succumbed. Moreover, he knows very well that the preaching of even the worthiest precepts only provokes the patient into open hostility or secret resistance and thus needlessly endangers the aim of the treatment. The psychic situation of the individual is so menaced nowadays by advertising, propaganda, and other more or less well-meant advice and suggestions that for once in his life the patient might be offered a relationship that does not repeat the nauseating "you should," "you must" and similar confessions of impotence. Against the onslaught from outside no less than against its repercussions in the psyche of the individual the analyst sees himself obliged to play the role of counsel for the defence. Fear that anarchic instincts will thereby be let loose is a possibility that

is greatly exaggerated, seeing that obvious safeguards exist within and without. Above all, there is the natural cowardice of most men to be reckoned with, not to mention morality, good taste and—last but not least—the penal code. This fear is nothing compared with the enormous effort it usually costs people to help the first stirrings of individuality into consciousness, let alone put them into effect. And where these individual impulses have broken through too boldly and unthinkingly, the analyst must protect them from the patient's own clumsy recourse to shortsightedness, ruthlessness, and cynicism.

535 As the dialectical discussion proceeds, a point is reached when an evaluation of these individual impulses becomes necessary. By that time the patient should have acquired enough certainty of judgment to enable him to act on his own insight and decision and not from the mere wish to copy convention—even if he happens to agree with collective opinion. Unless he stands firmly on his own feet, the so-called objective values profit him nothing, since they then only serve as a substitute for character and so help to suppress his individuality. Naturally, society has an indisputable right to protect itself against arrant subjectivisms, but, in so far as society is itself composed of de-individualized human beings, it is completely at the mercy of ruthless individualists. Let it band together into groups and organizations as much as it likes—it is just this banding together and the resultant extinction of the individual personality that makes it succumb so readily to a dictator. A million zeros joined together do not, unfortunately, add up to one. Ultimately everything depends on the quality of the individual, but our fatally shortsighted age thinks only in terms of large numbers and mass organizations, though one would think that the world had seen more than enough of what a well-disciplined mob can do in the hands of a single madman. Unfortunately, this realization does not seem to have penetrated very far—and our blindness is extremely dangerous. People go on blithely organizing and believing in the sovereign remedy of mass action, without the least consciousness of the fact that the most powerful organizations can be maintained only by the greatest ruthlessness of their leaders and the cheapest of slogans.

536 Curiously enough, the Churches too want to avail themselves of mass action in order to cast out the devil with Beelzebub—the

very Churches whose care is the salvation of the *individual* soul. They do not appear to have heard of the elementary axiom of mass psychology that the individual becomes morally and spiritually inferior in the mass, and for this reason they do not bother themselves overmuch with their real task of helping the individual to achieve a *metanoia,* a rebirth of the spirit—*Deo concedente.* It is, unfortunately, only too clear that if the individual is not truly regenerated in spirit, society cannot be either, for society is the sum total of individuals in need of redemption. I can therefore see it only as a delusion when the Churches try —as they apparently do—to rope the individual into some social organization and reduce him to a condition of diminished responsibility, instead of raising him out of the torpid, mindless mass and making clear to him that *he* is the one important factor and that the salvation of the world consists in the salvation of the individual soul. It is true that mass meetings parade these ideas before him and seek to impress them on his mind by dint of mass suggestion, with the melancholy result that once the intoxication has worn off the mass man promptly succumbs to another even more obvious and still louder slogan. His individual relation to God would be an effective shield against these pernicious influences. Did Christ, perchance, call his disciples to him at a mass meeting? Did the feeding of the five thousand bring him any followers who did not afterwards cry with the rest, "Crucify him!" when even the rock named Peter showed signs of wavering? And are not Jesus and Paul prototypes of those who, trusting their inner experience, have gone their individual ways in defiance of the world?

537   This argument should certainly not cause us to overlook the reality of the situation confronting the Church. When the Church tries to give shape to the amorphous mass by uniting individuals into a community of believers and to hold such an organization together with the help of suggestion, it is not only performing a great *social* service, but it also secures for the individual the inestimable boon of a meaningful form of life. These, however, are gifts which as a rule only confirm certain tendencies and do not change them. As experience unfortunately shows, the inner man remains unchanged however much community he has. His environment cannot give him as a gift something which he can win for himself only with effort and

suffering. On the contrary, a favourable environment merely strengthens the dangerous tendency to expect everything from outside—even that metamorphosis which external reality cannot provide. By this I mean a far-reaching change of the inner man, which is all the more urgent in view of the mass phenomena of today and the still greater problems of overpopulation looming in the future. It is time we asked ourselves exactly what we are lumping together in mass organizations and what constitutes the nature of the individual human being, i.e., of the real man and not the statistical man. This is hardly possible except by a new process of self-reflection.

538    All mass movements, as one might expect, slip with the greatest ease down an inclined plane made up of large numbers. Where the many are, there is security; what the many believe must of course be true; what the many want must be worth striving for, and necessary, and therefore good. In the clamour of the many resides the power to snatch wish-fulfilments by force; sweetest of all, however, is that gentle and painless slipping back into the kingdom of childhood, into the paradise of parental care, into happy-go-luckiness and irresponsibility. All the thinking and looking after are done from the top; to all questions there is an answer, and for all needs the necessary provision is made. The infantile dream-state of the mass man is so unrealistic that he never thinks to ask who is paying for this paradise. The balancing of accounts is left to a higher political or social authority, which welcomes the task, for its power is thereby increased; and the more power it has, the weaker and more helpless the individual becomes.

539    Whenever social conditions of this type develop on a large scale, the road to tyranny lies open and the freedom of the individual turns into spiritual and physical slavery. Since every tyranny is *ipso facto* immoral and ruthless, it has much more freedom in the choice of its methods than an institution which still takes account of the individual. Should such an institution come into conflict with the organized State, it is soon made aware of the very real disadvantage of its morality and therefore feels compelled to avail itself of the same methods as its opponent. In this way the evil spreads almost of necessity, even when direct infection might be avoided. The danger of infection is greater when decisive importance is attached to large numbers

33

and to statistical values, as is everywhere the case in our Western world. The suffocating power of the masses is paraded before our eyes in one form or another every day in the newspapers, and the insignificance of the individual is rubbed into him so thoroughly that he loses all hope of making himself heard. The outworn ideals of *liberté, égalité, fraternité* help him not at all, as he can direct this appeal only to his executioners, the spokesmen of the masses.

540   *Resistance to the organized mass can be effected only by the man who is as well organized in his individuality as the mass itself.* I fully realize that this proposition must sound well-nigh unintelligible to the man of today. The helpful medieval view that man is a microcosm, a reflection of the great cosmos in miniature, has long since dropped away from him, although the very existence of his world-embracing and world-conditioning psyche might have taught him better. Not only is the image of the macrocosm imprinted upon his psychic nature, but he also creates this image for himself on an ever-widening scale. He bears this cosmic "correspondence" within him by virtue of his reflecting consciousness on the one hand, and, on the other, thanks to the hereditary, archetypal nature of his instincts, which bind him to his environment. But his instincts not only attach him to the macrocosm, they also, in a sense, tear him apart, because his desires pull him in different directions. In this way he falls into continual conflict with himself and only very rarely succeeds in giving his life an undivided goal—for which, as a rule, he must pay very dearly by repressing other sides of his nature. One often has to ask oneself whether this kind of single-mindedness is worth forcing at all, seeing that the natural state of the human psyche consists in a jostling together of its components and in their contradictory behaviour—that is, in a certain degree of dissociation. The Buddhist name for this is attachment to the "ten thousand things." Such a condition cries out for order and synthesis.

541   Just as the chaotic movements of the crowd, all ending in mutual frustration, are impelled in a definite direction by a dictatorial will, so the individual in his dissociated state needs a directing and ordering principle. Ego-consciousness would like to let its own will play this role, but overlooks the existence of powerful unconscious factors which thwart its intentions. If it

wants to reach the goal of synthesis, it must first get to know the nature of these factors. It must *experience* them, or else it must possess a numinous *symbol* that expresses them and leads to their synthesis. A religious symbol that comprehended and visibly represented what is seeking expression in modern man might possibly do this; but our conception of the Christian symbol to date has certainly not been able to do so. On the contrary, that frightful world split runs right through the domains of the "Christian" white man, and our Christian outlook on life has proved powerless to prevent the recrudescence of an archaic social order like Communism.

542     This is not to say that Christianity is finished. I am, on the contrary, convinced that it is not Christianity, but our conception and interpretation of it, that has become antiquated in face of the present world situation. The Christian symbol is a living thing that carries in itself the seeds of further development. It can go on developing; it depends only on us, whether we can make up our minds to meditate again, and more thoroughly, on the Christian premises. This requires a very different attitude towards the individual, towards the microcosm of the self, from the one we have adopted hitherto. That is why nobody knows what ways of approach are open to man, what inner experiences he could still pass through and what psychic facts underlie the religious myth. Over all this hangs so universal a darkness that no one can see why he should be interested or to what end he should commit himself. Before this problem we stand helpless.

543     This is not surprising, since practically all the trump cards are in the hands of our opponents. They can appeal to the big battalions and their crushing power. Politics, science, and technology stand ranged on their side. The imposing arguments of science represent the highest degree of intellectual certainty yet achieved by the mind of man. So at least it seems to the man of today, who has received hundred-fold enlightenment concerning the backwardness and darkness of past ages and their superstitions. That his teachers have themselves gone seriously astray by making false comparisons between incommensurable factors never enters his head. All the more so as the intellectual *élite* to whom he puts his questions are almost unanimously agreed that what science regards as impossible today was impossible at all other times as well. Above all, the facts of faith, which might

35

give him the chance of an extramundane standpoint, are treated in the same context as the facts of science. Thus, when the individual questions the Churches and their spokesmen, to whom is entrusted the cure of souls, he is informed that to belong to a church—a decidedly worldly institution—is more or less *de rigueur;* that the facts of faith which have become questionable for him were concrete historical events; that certain ritual actions produce miraculous effects; and that the sufferings of Christ have vicariously saved him from sin and its consequences (i.e., eternal damnation). If, with the limited means at his disposal, he begins to reflect on these things, he will have to confess that he does not understand them at all and that only two possibilities remain open to him: either to believe implicitly, or to reject such statements because they are flatly incomprehensible.

544 Whereas the man of today can easily think about and understand all the "truths" dished out to him by the State, his understanding of religion is made considerably more difficult owing to the lack of explanations. ("Do you understand what you are reading?" And he said, "How can I, unless someone guides me?" Acts 8 : 30.) If, despite this, he has still not discarded all his religious convictions, this is because the religious impulse rests on an instinctive basis and is therefore a specifically human function. You can take away a man's gods, but only to give him others in return. The leaders of the mass State could not help being deified, and wherever crudities of this kind have not yet been put over by force, obsessive factors arise in their stead, charged with demonic energy—money, work, political influence, and so forth. When any natural human function gets lost, i.e., is denied conscious and intentional expression, a general disturbance results. Hence, it is quite natural that with the triumph of the Goddess of Reason a general neuroticizing of modern man should set in, a dissociation of personality analogous to the splitting of the world today by the Iron Curtain. This boundary line bristling with barbed wire runs through the psyche of modern man, no matter on which side he lives. And just as the typical neurotic is unconscious of his *shadow side,* so the normal individual, like the neurotic, sees his shadow in his neighbour or in the man beyond the great divide. It has even become a political and social duty to apostrophize the capitalism

of the one and the communism of the other as the very devil, so as to fascinate the outward eye and prevent it from looking within. But just as the neurotic, despite unconsciousness of his other side, has a dim premonition that all is not well with his psychic economy, so Western man has developed an instinctive interest in his psyche and in "psychology."

545 Thus it is that the psychiatrist is summoned willy-nilly to appear on the world stage, and questions are addressed to him which primarily concern the most intimate and hidden life of the individual, but which in the last analysis are the direct effects of the *Zeitgeist*. Because of its personal symptomatology this material is usually considered to be "neurotic"—and rightly so, since it is made up of infantile fantasies which ill accord with the contents of an adult psyche and are therefore repressed by our moral judgment, in so far as they reach consciousness at all. Most fantasies of this kind do not, in the nature of things, come to consciousness in any form, and it is very improbable, to say the least of it, that they were ever conscious and were consciously repressed. Rather, they seem to have been present from the beginning or, at any rate, to have arisen unconsciously and to have persisted in that state until the psychologist's intervention enabled them to cross the threshold of consciousness. The activation of unconscious fantasies is a process that occurs when consciousness finds itself in a situation of distress. Were that not so, the fantasies would be produced normally and would then bring no neurotic disturbances in their train. In reality, fantasies of this kind belong to the world of childhood and give rise to disturbances only when prematurely strengthened by abnormal conditions of conscious life. This is particularly likely to happen when unfavourable influences emanate from the parents, poisoning the atmosphere and producing conflicts which upset the psychic balance of the child.

546 When a neurosis breaks out in an adult, the fantasy world of childhood reappears, and one is tempted to explain the onset of the neurosis causally, as due to the presence of infantile fantasies. But that does not explain why the fantasies did not develop any pathological effects during the interim period. These effects develop only when the individual is faced with a situation which he cannot overcome by conscious means. The resultant standstill in the development of personality opens a sluice

37

for infantile fantasies, which, of course, are latent in everybody but do not display any activity so long as the conscious personality can continue on its way unimpeded. When the fantasies reach a certain level of intensity, they begin to break through into consciousness and create a conflict situation that becomes perceptible to the patient himself, splitting him into two personalities with different characters. The dissociation, however, had been prepared long before in the unconscious, when the energy flowing off from consciousness (because unused) reinforced the negative qualities of the unconscious and particularly the infantile traits of the personality.

547    Since the normal fantasies of a child are nothing other, at bottom, than the *imagination of the instincts,* and may thus be regarded as preliminary exercises in the use of future conscious activities, it follows that the fantasies of the neurotic, even though pathologically altered and perhaps perverted by the regression of energy, contain a core of normal instinct, the hallmark of which is adaptedness. A neurotic illness always implies an unadapted alteration and distortion of normal dynamisms and of the "imagination" proper to them. Instincts, however, are highly conservative and of extreme antiquity as regards both their dynamism and their form. Their form, when represented to the mind, appears as an *image* which expresses the nature of the instinctive impulse visually and concretely, like a picture. If we could look into the psyche of the yucca moth,[1] for instance, we would find in it a pattern of ideas, of a numinous or fascinating character, which not only compels the moth to carry out its fertilizing activity on the yucca plant but helps it to "recognize" the total situation. Instinct is anything but a blind and indefinite impulse, since it proves to be attuned and adapted to a definite external situation. This latter circumstance gives it its specific and irreducible form. Just as instinct is original and hereditary, so, too, its form is age-old, that is to say, *archetypal.* It is even older and more conservative than the body's form.

548    These biological considerations naturally apply also to *Homo sapiens,* who still remains within the framework of gen-

[1] This is a classic instance of the symbiosis of insect and plant. [Cf. "Instinct and the Unconscious," *The Structure and Dynamics of the Psyche,* pars. 268, 277.—EDITORS (1964).]

eral biology despite the possession of consciousness, will, and reason. The fact that our conscious activity is rooted in instinct and derives from it its dynamism as well as the basic features of its ideational forms has the same significance for human psychology as for all other members of the animal kingdom. Human knowledge consists essentially in the constant adaptation of the primordial patterns of ideas that were given us *a priori*. These need certain modifications, because, in their original form, they are suited to an archaic mode of life but not to the demands of a specifically differentiated environment. If the flow of instinctive dynamism into our life is to be maintained, as is absolutely necessary for our existence, then it is imperative that we should remould these archetypal forms into ideas which are adequate to the challenge of the present.

# 5. THE PHILOSOPHICAL AND THE PSYCHOLOGICAL APPROACH TO LIFE

549    Our ideas have, however, the unfortunate but inevitable tendency to lag behind the changes in the total situation. They can hardly do otherwise, because, so long as nothing changes in the world, they remain more or less adapted and therefore function in a satisfactory way. There is then no cogent reason why they should be changed and adapted anew. Only when conditions have altered so drastically that there is an unendurable rift between the outer situation and our ideas, now become antiquated, does the general problem of our *Weltanschauung*, or philosophy of life, arise, and with it the question of how the primordial images that maintain the flow of instinctive energy are to be reoriented or readapted. They cannot simply be replaced by a new rational configuration, for this would be moulded too much by the outward situation and not enough by man's biological needs. Moreover, not only would it build no bridge to the original man, but it would block the approach to him altogether. This is in keeping with the aims of Marxist education, which seeks, like God himself, to remake man, but in the image of the State.

550    Today, our basic convictions are becoming increasingly rationalistic. Our philosophy is no longer a way of life, as it was in antiquity; it has turned into an exclusively intellectual and academic exercise. Our denominational religions with their archaic rites and conceptions—justified enough in themselves—express a view of the world which caused no great difficulties in the Middle Ages but has become strange and unintelligible to modern man. Despite this conflict with the modern scientific outlook, a deep instinct bids him hang on to ideas which, if taken literally, leave out of account all the mental developments of the last five hundred years. The obvious purpose of this is to prevent him from falling into the abyss of nihilistic despair. But

even when, as a rationalist, he feels impelled to criticize denominational religion as literalistic, narrow-minded, and obsolescent, he should never forget that it proclaims a doctrine whose symbols, although their interpretation may be disputed, nevertheless possess a life of their own by virtue of their archetypal character. Consequently, intellectual understanding is by no means indispensable in all cases, but is called for only when evaluation through feeling and intuition does not suffice, that is to say, in the case of people for whom the intellect carries the prime power of conviction.

551 Nothing is more characteristic and symptomatic in this respect than the gulf that has opened out between *faith* and *knowledge.* The contrast has become so enormous that one is obliged to speak of the incommensurability of these two categories and their way of looking at the world. And yet they are concerned with the same empirical world in which we live, for even the theologians tell us that faith is supported by facts that became historically perceptible in this known world of ours—namely that Christ was born as a real human being, worked many miracles and suffered his fate, died under Pontius Pilate, and rose up in the flesh after his death. Theology rejects any tendency to take the assertions of its earliest records as written myths and, accordingly, to understand them symbolically. Indeed, it is the theologians themselves who have recently made the attempt—no doubt as a concession to "knowledge"—to "demythologize" the object of their faith while drawing the line quite arbitrarily at the crucial points. But to the critical intellect it is only too obvious that myth is an integral component of all religions and therefore cannot be excluded from the assertions of faith without injuring them.

552 The rupture between faith and knowledge is a symptom of the *split consciousness* which is so characteristic of the mental disorder of our day. It is as if two different persons were making statements about the same thing, each from his own point of view, or as if one person in two different frames of mind were sketching a picture of his experience. If for "person" we substitute "modern society," it is evident that the latter is suffering from a mental dissociation, i.e., a neurotic disturbance. In view of this, it does not help matters at all if one party pulls obstinately to the right and the other to the left. This is what hap-

pens in every neurotic psyche, to its own deep distress, and it is just this distress that brings the patient to the analyst.

553 As I stated above in all brevity—while not neglecting to mention certain practical details whose omission might have perplexed the reader—the analyst has to establish a relationship with *both* halves of his patient's personality, because only from them can he put together a whole and complete man, and not merely from one half by suppression of the other half. But this suppression is just what the patient has been doing all along, for the modern *Weltanschauung* leaves him with no alternative. His individual situation is the same in principle as the collective situation. He is a social microcosm, reflecting on the smallest scale the qualities of society at large, or conversely the smallest social unit cumulatively producing the collective dissociation. The latter possibility is the more likely one, as the only direct and concrete carrier of life is the individual personality, while society and the State are conventional ideas and can claim reality only in so far as they are represented by a conglomeration of individuals.

554 Far too little attention has been paid to the fact that, for all our irreligiousness, the distinguishing mark of the Christian epoch, its highest achievement, has become the congenital vice of our age: *the supremacy of the word,* of the Logos, which stands for the central figure of our Christian faith. The word has literally become our god and so it has remained, even if we know of Christianity only from hearsay. Words like "Society" and "State" are so concretized that they are almost personified. In the opinion of the man in the street, the "State," far more than any king in history, is the inexhaustible giver of all good; the "State" is invoked, made responsible, grumbled at, and so on and so forth. Society is elevated to the rank of a supreme ethical principle; indeed, it is even credited with positively creative capacities. No one seems to notice that this worship of the word, which was necessary at a certain phase of man's mental development, has a perilous shadow side. That is to say, the moment the word, as a result of centuries of education, attains universal validity, it severs its original connection with the divine Person. There is then a personified Church, a personified State; belief in the word becomes credulity, and the word itself an infernal slogan capable of any deception. With credulity

come propaganda and advertising to dupe the citizen with political jobbery and compromises, and the lie reaches proportions never known before in the history of the world.

555    Thus the word, originally announcing the unity of all men and their union in the figure of the one great Man, has in our day become a source of suspicion and distrust of all against all. Credulity is one of our worst enemies, but that is the makeshift the neurotic always resorts to in order to quell the doubter in his own breast or to conjure him out of existence. People think you have only to "tell" a person that he "ought" to do something in order to put him on the right track. But whether he can or will do it is another matter. The psychologist has come to see that nothing is achieved by telling, persuading, admonishing, giving good advice. He must acquaint himself with all the particulars and have an authentic knowledge of the psychic inventory of his patient. He has therefore to relate to the individuality of the sufferer and feel his way into all the nooks and crannies of his mind, to a degree that far exceeds the capacity of a teacher or even of a *directeur de conscience*. His scientific objectivity, which excludes nothing, enables him to see his patient not only as a human being but also as an anthropoid, who is bound to his body like an animal. His training directs his medical interest beyond the conscious personality to the world of unconscious instinct dominated by sexuality and the power drive (or self-assertion), which correspond to the twin moral concepts of Saint Augustine: *concupiscentia* and *superbia*. The clash between these two fundamental instincts (preservation of the species and self-preservation) is the source of numerous conflicts. They are, therefore, the chief object of moral judgment, whose purpose it is to prevent instinctual collisions as far as possible.

556    As I explained earlier, instinct has two main aspects: on the one hand, that of dynamism and compulsion, and on the other, specific meaning and intention. It is highly probable that all man's psychic functions have an instinctual foundation, as is obviously the case with animals. It is easy to see that in animals instinct functions as the *spiritus rector* of all behaviour. This observation lacks certainty only when the learning capacity begins to develop, for instance in the higher apes and in man. In animals, as a result of their learning capacity, instinct under-

43

goes numerous modifications and differentiations, and in civilized man the instincts are so split up that only a few of the basic ones can be recognized with any certainty in their original form. The most important are the two fundamental instincts already mentioned and their derivatives, and these have been the exclusive concern of medical psychology so far. But in following up the ramifications of instinct investigators came upon configurations which could not with certainty be ascribed to either group. To take but one example: The discoverer of the power instinct raised the question whether an apparently indubitable expression of the sexual instinct might not be better explained as a "power arrangement," and Freud himself felt obliged to acknowledge the existence of "ego instincts" in addition to the overriding sexual instinct—a clear concession to the Adlerian standpoint. In view of this uncertainty, it is hardly surprising that in most cases neurotic symptoms can be explained, almost without contradiction, in terms of either theory. This perplexity does not mean that one or the other standpoint is erroneous or that both are. Rather, both are *relatively* valid and, unlike certain one-sided and dogmatic tendencies, admit the existence and competition of still other instincts. Although, as I have said, the question of human instinct is a far from simple matter, we shall probably not be wrong in assuming that the learning capacity, a quality almost exclusive to man, is based on the instinct for imitation found in animals. It is in the nature of this instinct to disturb other instinctive activities and eventually to modify them, as can be observed, for instance, in the songs of birds when they adopt other melodies.

557    Nothing estranges man more from the ground-plan of his instincts than his learning capacity, which turns out to be a genuine drive for progressive transformation of human modes of behaviour. It, more than anything else, is responsible for the altered conditions of his existence and the need for new adaptations which civilization brings. It is also the ultimate source of those numerous psychic disturbances and difficulties which are occasioned by man's progressive alienation from his instinctual foundation, i.e., by his uprootedness and identification with his conscious knowledge of himself, by his concern with consciousness at the expense of the unconscious. The result is that modern man knows himself only in so far as he can become con-

scious of himself—a capacity largely dependent on environmental conditions, knowledge and control of which necessitated or suggested certain modifications of his original instinctive tendencies. His consciousness therefore orients itself chiefly by observing and investigating the world around him, and it is to the latter's peculiarities that he must adapt his psychic and technical resources. This task is so exacting, and its fulfilment so profitable, that he forgets himself in the process, losing sight of his instinctual nature and putting his own conception of himself in place of his real being. In this way he slips imperceptibly into a purely conceptual world where the products of his conscious activity progressively take the place of reality.

558    Separation from his instinctual nature inevitably plunges civilized man into the conflict between conscious and unconscious, spirit and nature, knowledge and faith, a split that becomes pathological the moment his consciousness is no longer able to neglect or suppress his instinctual side. The accumulation of individuals who have got into this critical state starts off a mass movement purporting to be the champion of the suppressed. In accordance with the prevailing tendency of consciousness to seek the source of all ills in the outside world, the cry goes up for political and social changes which, it is supposed, would automatically solve the much deeper problem of split personality. Hence it is that whenever this demand is fulfilled, political and social conditions arise which bring the same ills back again in altered form. What then happens is a simple reversal: the underside comes to the top and the shadow takes the place of the light, and since the former is always anarchic and turbulent, the freedom of the "liberated" underdog must suffer Draconian curtailment. The devil is cast out with Beelzebub. All this is unavoidable, because the root of the evil is untouched and merely the counterposition has come to light.

559    The Communist revolution has debased man far lower than democratic collective psychology has done, because it robs him of his freedom not only in the social but in the moral and spiritual sphere. Aside from the political difficulties, this entailed a great psychological disadvantage for the West that had already made itself unpleasantly felt in the days of German Nazism: we can now point a finger at the shadow. He is clearly on the other side of the political frontier, while we are on the side of

45

good and enjoy the possession of the right ideals. Did not a well-known statesman recently confess that he had "no imagination for evil"? [1] In the name of the multitude he was expressing the fact that Western man is in danger of losing his shadow altogether, of identifying himself with his fictive personality and the world with the abstract picture painted by scientific rationalism. His spiritual and moral opponent, who is just as real as he, no longer dwells in his own breast but beyond the geographical line of division, which no longer represents an outward political barrier but splits off the conscious from the unconscious man more and more menacingly. Thinking and feeling lose their inner polarity, and where religious orientation has grown ineffective, not even a god can check the sovereign sway of unleashed psychic functions.

560    Our rational philosophy does not bother itself with whether the other person in us, pejoratively described as the "shadow," is in sympathy with our conscious plans and intentions. Evidently it still does not know that we carry in ourselves a real shadow whose existence is grounded in our instinctual nature. No one can overlook either the dynamism or the imagery of the instincts without the gravest injury to himself. Violation or neglect of instinct has painful consequences of a physiological and psychological nature for whose treatment medical help, above all, is required.

561    For more than fifty years we have known, or could have known, that there is an unconscious counterbalance to consciousness. Medical psychology has furnished all the necessary empirical and experimental proofs of this. There is an unconscious psychic reality which demonstrably influences consciousness and its contents. All this is known, but no practical conclusions have been drawn from this fact. We still go on thinking and acting as before, as if we were *simplex* and not *duplex*. Accordingly, we imagine ourselves to be innocuous, reasonable, and humane. We do not think of distrusting our motives or of asking ourselves how the inner man feels about the things we do in the outside world. But actually it is frivolous, superficial, and unreasonable of us, as well as psychically unhygienic, to overlook the reaction and standpoint of the unconscious. One

---

[1] Since these words were written, the shadow has followed up this overbright picture hotfoot with the Charge of the Light Brigade to Suez [1956].

can regard one's stomach or heart as unimportant and worthy of contempt, but that does not prevent overeating or overexertion from having consequences that affect the whole man. Yet we think that psychic mistakes and their consequences can be got rid of with mere words, for "psychic" means less than air to most people. All the same, nobody can deny that without the psyche there would be no world at all, and still less a human world. Virtually everything depends on the human psyche and its functions. It should be worthy of all the attention we can give it, especially today, when everyone admits that the weal or woe of the future will be decided neither by the threat of wild animals, nor by natural catastrophes, nor by the danger of world-wide epidemics, but simply and solely by the psychic changes in man. It needs only an almost imperceptible disturbance of equilibrium in a few of our rulers' heads to plunge the world into blood, fire, and radioactivity. The technical means necessary for this are present on both sides. And certain conscious deliberations, uncontrolled by any inner opponent, can be put into effect all too easily, as we have seen already from the example of one "Leader." The consciousness of modern man still clings so much to external objects that he makes them exclusively responsible, as if it were on them that the decision depended. That the psychic state of certain individuals could ever emancipate itself from the behaviour of objects is something that is considered far too little, although irrationalities of this sort are observed every day and can happen to everyone.

562    The forlorn state of consciousness in our world is due primarily to loss of instinct, and the reason for this lies in the development of the human mind over the past aeon. The more power man had over nature, the more his knowledge and skill went to his head, and the deeper became his contempt for the merely natural and accidental, for all irrational data—including the objective psyche, which is everything that consciousness is not. In contrast to the subjectivism of the conscious mind the unconscious is objective, manifesting itself mainly in the form of contrary feelings, fantasies, emotions, impulses, and dreams, none of which one makes oneself but which come upon one objectively. Even today psychology is still, for the most part, the science of conscious contents, measured as far as possible by collective standards. The individual psyche has become a mere

accident, a marginal phenomenon, while the unconscious, which can manifest itself only in the real, "irrationally given" human being, has been ignored altogether. This was not the result of carelessness or of lack of knowledge, but of downright resistance to the mere possibility that there could be a second psychic authority besides the ego. It seems a positive menace to the ego that its monarchy could be doubted. The religious person, on the other hand, is accustomed to the thought of not being sole master in his own house. He believes that God, and not he himself, decides in the end. But how many of us would dare to let the will of God decide, and which of us would not feel embarrassed if he had to say how far the decision came from God himself?

563    The religious person, so far as one can judge, is directly influenced by the reaction of the unconscious. As a rule, he calls this the operation of *conscience*. But since the same psychic background produces reactions other than moral ones,[2] the believer is measuring his conscience by the traditional ethical standard and thus by a collective value, in which endeavour he is assiduously supported by his Church. So long as the individual can hold fast to his traditional beliefs, and the circumstances of his time do not demand stronger emphasis on individual autonomy, he can rest content with the situation. But the situation is radically altered when the worldly-minded man who is oriented to external factors and has lost his religious beliefs appears *en masse*, as is the case today. The believer is then forced onto the defensive and must catechize himself on the foundation of his beliefs. He is no longer sustained by the tremendous suggestive power of the *consensus omnium* and is keenly aware of the weakening of the Church and the precariousness of its dogmatic assumptions. To counter this, the Church recommends more faith, as if this gift of grace depended on man's good will and pleasure. The seat of faith, however, is not consciousness but spontaneous religious experience, which brings the individual's faith into immediate relation with God.

564    Here each of us must ask: Have I any religious experience and immediate relation to God, and hence that certainty which will keep me, as an individual, from dissolving in the crowd?

² [Cf. "A Psychological View of Conscience" (1958), CW 10, par. 826.—EDITORS (1964).]

# 6. SELF-KNOWLEDGE

565    To this question there is a positive answer only when the individual is willing to fulfil the demands of rigorous self-examination and self-knowledge. If he does this, he will not only discover some important truths about himself but will also have gained a psychological advantage: he will have succeeded in deeming himself worthy of serious attention and sympathetic interest. He will have set his hand, as it were, to a declaration of his own human dignity and taken the first step towards the foundations of his consciousness—that is, towards the unconscious, the only available source of religious experience. This is certainly not to say that what we call the unconscious is identical with God or is set up in his place. It is simply the medium from which religious experience seems to flow. As to what the further cause of such experience may be, the answer to this lies beyond the range of human knowledge. Knowledge of God is a transcendental problem.

566    The religious person enjoys a great advantage when it comes to answering the crucial question that hangs over our time like a threat: he has a clear idea of the way his subjective existence is grounded in his relation to "God." I put the word "God" in quotes in order to indicate that we are dealing with an anthropomorphic idea whose dynamism and symbolism are filtered through the medium of the unconscious psyche. Anyone who wants to can at least draw near to the source of such experiences, no matter whether he believes in God or not. Without this approach it is only in rare cases that we witness those miraculous conversions of which Paul's Damascus experience is the prototype. That religious experiences exist no longer needs proof. But it will always remain doubtful whether what metaphysics and theology call God and the gods is the real ground of these experiences. The question is idle, actually, and answers itself by reason of the subjectively overwhelming numinosity of

49

the experience. Anyone who has had it is *seized* by it and therefore not in a position to indulge in fruitless metaphysical or
epistemological speculations. Absolute certainty brings its own
evidence and has no need of anthropomorphic proofs.

567 In view of the general ignorance of and bias against psychology it must be accounted a misfortune that the one experience which makes sense of individual existence should seem to
have its origin in a medium that is certain to catch everybody's
prejudices. Once more the doubt is heard: "What good can
come out of Nazareth?" The unconscious, if not regarded outright as a sort of refuse bin underneath the conscious mind, is
at any rate supposed to be of "merely animal nature." In reality,
however, and by definition it is of uncertain extent and constitution, so that overvaluation or undervaluation of it is pointless
and can be dismissed as mere prejudice. At all events, such judgments sound very queer in the mouths of Christians, whose
Lord was himself born on the straw of a stable, among the
domestic animals. It would have been more to the taste of the
multitude if he had got himself born in a temple. In the same
way, the worldly-minded mass man looks for the numinous experience in the mass meeting, which provides an infinitely more
imposing background than the individual soul. Even Church
Christians share this pernicious delusion.

568 Psychology's insistence on the importance of unconscious
processes for religious experience is extremely unpopular, no
less with the political Right than with the Left. For the former
the deciding factor is the historical revelation that came to man
from outside; to the latter this is sheer nonsense, and man has
no religious function at all, except belief in the party doctrine,
when suddenly the most intense faith is called for. On top of
this, the various creeds assert quite different things, and each of
them claims to possess the absolute truth. Yet today we live in a
unitary world where distances are reckoned by hours and no
longer by weeks and months. Exotic races have ceased to be
peepshows in ethnological museums. They have become our
neighbours, and what was yesterday the private concern of the
ethnologist is today a political, social, and psychological problem. Already the ideological spheres begin to touch, to inter-
penetrate, and the time may not be far off when the question of
mutual understanding will become acute. To make oneself un-

derstood is certainly impossible without far-reaching comprehension of the other's standpoint. The insight needed for this will have repercussions on both sides. History will undoubtedly pass over those who feel it is their vocation to resist this inevitable development, however desirable and psychologically necessary it may be to cling to what is essential and good in our own tradition. Despite all the differences, the unity of mankind will assert itself irresistibly. On this card Marxist doctrine has staked its life, while the West hopes to achieve its aim with technology and economic aid. Communism has not overlooked the enormous importance of the ideological element and the universality of basic principles. The coloured races share our ideological weakness and in this respect are just as vulnerable as we are.

569    The underestimation of the psychological factor is likely to take a bitter revenge. It is therefore high time we caught up with ourselves in this matter. For the present this must remain a pious wish, because self-knowledge, as well as being highly unpopular, seems to be an unpleasantly idealistic goal, reeks of morality, and is preoccupied with the psychological shadow, which is normally denied whenever possible or at least not spoken of. The task that faces our age is indeed almost insuperably difficult. It makes the highest demands on our responsibility if we are not to be guilty of another *trahison des clercs*. It addresses itself to those leading and influential personalities who have the necessary intelligence to understand the situation our world is in. One might expect them to consult their consciences. But since it is a matter not only of intellectual understanding but of moral conclusions, there is unfortunately no cause for optimism. Nature, as we know, is not so lavish with her boons that she joins to a high intelligence the gifts of the heart also. As a rule, where one is present the other is missing, and where one capacity is present in perfection it is generally at the cost of all the others. The discrepancy between intellect and feeling, which get in each other's way at the best of times, is a particularly painful chapter in the history of the human psyche.

570    There is no sense in formulating the task that our age has forced upon us as a moral demand. We can, at best, merely make the psychological world situation so clear that it can be

seen even by the myopic, and give utterance to words and ideas which even the hard of hearing can hear. We may hope for men of understanding and men of good will, and must therefore not grow weary of reiterating those thoughts and insights which are needed. Finally, even the truth can spread and not only the popular lie.

571    With these words I should like to draw the reader's attention to the main difficulty he has to face. The horror which the dictator States have of late brought upon mankind is nothing less than the culmination of all those atrocities of which our ancestors made themselves guilty in the not so distant past. Quite apart from the barbarities and blood baths perpetrated by the Christian nations among themselves throughout European history, the European has also to answer for all the crimes he has committed against the coloured races during the process of colonization. In this respect the white man carries a very heavy burden indeed. It shows us a picture of the common human shadow that could hardly be painted in blacker colours. The evil that comes to light in man and that undoubtedly dwells within him is of gigantic proportions, so that for the Church to talk of original sin and to trace it back to Adam's relatively innocent slip-up with Eve is almost a euphemism. The case is far graver and is grossly underestimated.

572    Since it is universally believed that man *is* merely what his consciousness knows of itself, he regards himself as harmless and so adds stupidity to iniquity. He does not deny that terrible things have happened and still go on happening, but it is always "the others" who do them. And when such deeds belong to the recent or remote past, they quickly and conveniently sink into the sea of forgetfulness, and that state of chronic woolly-mindedness returns which we describe as "normality." In shocking contrast to this is the fact that nothing has finally disappeared and nothing has been made good. The evil, the guilt, the profound unease of conscience, the dark foreboding, are there before our eyes, if only we would see. Man has done these things; I am a man, who has his share of human nature; therefore I am guilty with the rest and bear unaltered and indelibly within me the capacity and the inclination to do them again at any time. Even if, juristically speaking, we were not accessories to the crime, we are always, thanks to our human nature, potential criminals. In

reality we merely lacked a suitable opportunity to be drawn into the infernal mêlée. None of us stands outside humanity's black collective shadow. Whether the crime occurred many generations back or happens today, it remains the symptom of a disposition that is always and everywhere present—and one would therefore do well to possess some "imagination for evil," for only the fool can permanently disregard the conditions of his own nature. In fact, this negligence is the best means of making him an instrument of evil. Harmlessness and naïveté are as little helpful as it would be for a cholera patient and those in his vicinity to remain unconscious of the contagiousness of the disease. On the contrary, they lead to projection of the unrecognized evil into the "other." This strengthens the opponent's position in the most effective way, because the projection carries the *fear* which we involuntarily and secretly feel for our own evil over to the other side and considerably increases the formidableness of his threat. What is even worse, our lack of insight deprives us of the *capacity to deal with evil.* Here, of course, we come up against one of the main prejudices of the Christian tradition, and one that is a great stumbling block to our policies. We should, so we are told, eschew evil and, if possible, neither touch nor mention it. For evil is also the thing of ill omen, that which is tabooed and feared. This apotropaic attitude towards evil, and the apparent circumventing of it, flatter the primitive tendency in us to shut our eyes to evil and drive it over some frontier or other, like the Old Testament scapegoat, which was supposed to carry the evil into the wilderness.

573    But if one can no longer avoid the realization that evil, without man's ever having chosen it, is lodged in human nature itself, then it bestrides the psychological stage as the equal and opposite partner of good. This realization leads straight to a psychological dualism, already unconsciously prefigured in the political world schism and in the even more unconscious dissociation in modern man himself. The dualism does not come from this realization; rather, we are in a split condition to begin with. It would be an insufferable thought that we had to take personal responsibility for so much guiltiness. We therefore prefer to localize the evil in individual criminals or groups of criminals, while washing our hands in innocence and ignoring the general proclivity to evil. This sanctimoniousness cannot be

kept up in the long run, because the evil, as experience shows, lies in man—unless, in accordance with the Christian view, one is willing to postulate a metaphysical principle of evil. The great advantage of this view is that it exonerates man's conscience of too heavy a responsibility and foists it off on the devil, in correct psychological appreciation of the fact that man is much more the victim of his psychic constitution than its inventor. Considering that the evil of our day puts everything that has ever agonized mankind in the deepest shade, one must ask oneself how it is that, for all our progress in the administration of justice, in medicine and in technology, for all our concern with life and health, monstrous engines of destruction have been invented which could easily exterminate the human race.

574     No one will maintain that the atomic physicists are a pack of criminals because it is to their efforts that we owe that peculiar flower of human ingenuity, the hydrogen bomb. The vast amount of intellectual work that went into the development of nuclear physics was put forth by men who dedicated themselves to their task with the greatest exertion and self-sacrifice, and whose moral achievement could therefore just as easily have earned them the merit of inventing something useful and beneficial to humanity. But even though the first step along the road to a momentous invention may be the outcome of a conscious decision, here, as everywhere, the spontaneous idea—the hunch or intuition—plays an important part. In other words, the unconscious collaborates too and often makes decisive contributions. So it is not the conscious effort alone that is responsible for the result; somewhere or other the unconscious, with its barely discernible goals and intentions, has its finger in the pie. If it puts a weapon in your hand, it is aiming at some kind of violence. Knowledge of the truth is the foremost goal of science, and if in pursuit of the longing for light we stumble upon an immense danger, then one has the impression more of fatality than of premeditation. It is not that present-day man is capable of greater evil than the man of antiquity or the primitive. He merely has incomparably more effective means with which to realize his propensity to evil. As his consciousness has broadened and differentiated, so his moral nature has lagged behind. That is the great problem before us today. *Reason alone no longer suffices.*

575    In theory, it lies within the power of reason to desist from experiments of such hellish scope as nuclear fission if only because of their dangerousness. But fear of the evil which one does not see in one's own bosom but always in somebody else's checks reason every time, although everyone knows that the use of this weapon means the certain end of our present human world. The fear of universal destruction may spare us the worst, yet the possibility of it will nevertheless hang over us like a dark cloud so long as no bridge is found across the world-wide psychic and political split—a bridge as certain as the existence of the hydrogen bomb. If only a world-wide consciousness could arise that all division and all fission are due to the splitting of opposites in the psyche, then we should know where to begin. But if even the smallest and most personal stirrings of the individual psyche—so insignificant in themselves—remain as unconscious and unrecognized as they have hitherto, they will go on accumulating and produce mass groupings and mass movements which cannot be subjected to reasonable control or manipulated to a good end. All direct efforts to do so are no more than shadow boxing, the most infatuated by illusion being the gladiators themselves.

576    The crux of the matter is man's own dualism, to which he knows no answer. This abyss has suddenly yawned open before him with the latest events in world history, after mankind had lived for many centuries in the comfortable belief that a unitary God had created man in his own image, as a little unity. Even today people are largely unconscious of the fact that every individual is a cell in the structure of various international organisms and is therefore causally implicated in their conflicts. He knows that as an individual being he is more or less meaningless and feels himself the victim of uncontrollable forces, but, on the other hand, he harbours within himself a dangerous shadow and adversary who is involved as an invisible helper in the dark machinations of the political monster. It is in the nature of political bodies always to see the evil in the opposite group, just as the individual has an ineradicable tendency to get rid of everything he does not know and does not want to know about himself.by foisting it off on somebody else.

577    Nothing has a more divisive and alienating effect upon society than this moral complacency and lack of responsibility,

55

and nothing promotes understanding and *rapprochement* more than the mutual withdrawal of projections. This necessary corrective demands self-criticism, for one cannot just tell the other person to withdraw them. He does not recognize them for what they are any more than one does oneself. We can recognize our prejudices and illusions only when, from a broader psychological knowledge of ourselves and others, we are prepared to doubt the absolute rightness of our assumptions and compare them carefully and conscientiously with the objective facts. Funnily enough, "self-criticism" is an idea much in vogue in Marxist countries, but there it is subordinated to ideological considerations and must serve the State, and not truth and justice in men's dealings with one another. The mass State has no intention of promoting mutual understanding and the relationship of man to man; it strives, rather, for atomization, for the psychic isolation of the individual. The more unrelated individuals are, the more consolidated the State becomes, and vice versa.

578    There can be no doubt that in the democracies too the distance between man and man is much greater than is conducive to public welfare, let alone beneficial to our psychic needs. True, all sorts of attempts are being made to level out glaring social contrasts by appealing to people's idealism, enthusiasm, and ethical conscience; but, characteristically, one forgets to apply the necessary self-criticism, to answer the question: *Who* is making the idealistic demand? Is it, perchance, someone who jumps over his own shadow in order to hurl himself avidly on some idealistic programme that offers him a welcome alibi? How much respectability and apparent morality is there, cloaking in deceptive colours a very different inner world of darkness? One would first like to be assured that the man who talks of ideals is himself ideal, so that his words and deeds *are* more than they *seem*. To be ideal is impossible, and remains therefore an unfulfilled postulate. Since we usually have keen noses in this respect, most of the idealisms that are preached and paraded before us sound rather hollow and become acceptable only when their opposite is also openly admitted. Without this counterweight the ideal exceeds our human capacity, becomes incredible because of its humourlessness, and degenerates into bluff, albeit a well-meant one. Bluff is an illegitimate way of

overpowering and suppressing others and leads to no good.

579     Recognition of the shadow, on the other hand, leads to the modesty we need in order to acknowledge imperfection. And it is just this conscious recognition and consideration that are needed whenever a human relationship is to be established. A human relationship is not based on differentiation and perfection, for these only emphasize the differences or call forth the exact opposite; it is based, rather, on imperfection, on what is weak, helpless and in need of support—the very ground and motive for dependence. The perfect have no need of others, but weakness has, for it seeks support and does not confront its partner with anything that might force him into an inferior position and even humiliate him. This humiliation may happen only too easily when high idealism plays too prominent a role.

580     Reflections of this kind should not be taken as superfluous sentimentalities. The question of human relationship and of the inner cohesion of our society is an urgent one in view of the atomization of the pent-up mass man, whose personal relationships are undermined by general mistrust. Wherever justice is uncertain and police spying and terror are at work, human beings fall into isolation, which, of course, is the aim and purpose of the dictator State, since it is based on the greatest possible accumulation of depotentiated social units. To counter this danger, the free society needs a bond of an affective nature, a principle of a kind like *caritas*, the Christian love of your neighbour. But it is just this love for one's fellow man that suffers most of all from the lack of understanding wrought by projection. It would therefore be very much in the interest of the free society to give some thought to the question of human relationship from the psychological point of view, for in this resides its real cohesion and consequently its strength. Where love stops, power begins, and violence, and terror.

581     These reflections are not intended as an appeal to idealism, but only to promote a consciousness of the psychological situation. I do not know which is weaker: the idealism or the insight of the public. I only know that it needs time to bring about psychic changes that have any prospect of enduring. Insight that dawns slowly seems to me to have more lasting effects than a fitful idealism, which is unlikely to hold out for long.

## 7. THE MEANING OF SELF-KNOWLEDGE

582    What our age thinks of as the "shadow" and inferior part of the psyche contains more than something merely negative. The very fact that through self-knowledge, that is, by exploring our own souls, we come upon the instincts and their world of imagery should throw some light on the powers slumbering in the psyche, of which we are seldom aware so long as all goes well. They are potentialities of the greatest dynamism, and it depends entirely on the preparedness and attitude of the conscious mind whether the irruption of these forces, and the images and ideas associated with them, will tend towards construction or catastrophe. The psychologist seems to be the only person who knows from experience how precarious the psychic preparedness of modern man is, for he is the only one who sees himself compelled to seek out in man's own nature those helpful powers and ideas which over and over have enabled him to find the right way through darkness and danger. For this exacting work the psychologist requires all his patience; he may not rely on any traditional oughts and musts, leaving the other person to make all the effort and contenting himself with the easy role of adviser and admonisher. Everyone knows the futility of preaching about things that are desirable, yet the general helplessness in this situation is so great, and the need so dire, that one prefers to repeat the old mistake instead of racking one's brains over a subjective problem. Besides, it is always a question of treating one single individual only and not ten thousand, when the trouble one takes would ostensibly have more impressive results, though one knows well enough that nothing has happened at all unless the individual changes.

583    The effect on *all* individuals, which one would like to see realized, may not set in for hundreds of years, for the spiritual transformation of mankind follows the slow tread of the cen-

turies and cannot be hurried or held up by any rational process of reflection, let alone brought to fruition in one generation. What does lie within our reach, however, is the change in individuals who have, or create for themselves, an opportunity to influence others of like mind. I do not mean by persuading or preaching—I am thinking, rather, of the well-known fact that anyone who has insight into his own actions, and has thus found access to the unconscious, involuntarily exercises an influence on his environment. The deepening and broadening of his consciousness produce the kind of effect which the primitives call "mana." It is an unintentional influence on the unconscious of others, a sort of unconscious prestige, and its effect lasts only so long as it is not disturbed by conscious intention.

584     Nor is the striving for self-knowledge altogether without prospects of success, since there exists a factor which, though completely disregarded, meets our expectations halfway. This is the unconscious *Zeitgeist*. It compensates the attitude of the conscious mind and anticipates changes to come. An excellent example of this is modern art: though seeming to deal with aesthetic problems, it is really performing a work of psychological education on the public by breaking down and destroying their previous aesthetic views of what is beautiful in form and meaningful in content. The pleasingness of the artistic product is replaced by chill abstractions of the most subjective nature which brusquely slam the door on the naïve and romantic delight in the senses and on the obligatory love for the object. This tells us, in plain and universal language, that the prophetic spirit of art has turned away from the old object-relationship towards the—for the time being—dark chaos of subjectivisms. Certainly art, so far as we can judge of it, has not yet discovered in this darkness what it is that could hold all men together and give expression to their psychic wholeness. Since reflection seems to be needed for this purpose, it may be that such discoveries are reserved for other fields of endeavour.

585     Great art till now has always derived its fruitfulness from myth, from the unconscious process of symbolization which continues through the ages and, as the primordial manifestation of the human spirit, will continue to be the root of all creation in the future. The development of modern art with its seemingly nihilistic trend towards disintegration must be

understood as the symptom and symbol of a mood of universal destruction and renewal that has set its mark on our age. This mood makes itself felt everywhere, politically, socially, and philosophically. We are living in what the Greeks called the καιρός—the right moment—for a "metamorphosis of the gods," of the fundamental principles and symbols. This peculiarity of our time, which is certainly not of our conscious choosing, is the expression of the unconscious man within us who is changing. Coming generations will have to take account of this momentous transformation if humanity is not to destroy itself through the might of its own technology and science.

586    As at the beginning of the Christian era, so again today we are faced with the problem of the general moral backwardness which has failed to keep pace with our scientific, technical, and social progress. So much is at stake and so much depends on the psychological constitution of modern man. Is he capable of resisting the temptation to use his power for the purpose of staging a world conflagration? Is he conscious of the path he is treading, and what the conclusions are that must be drawn from the present world situation and his own psychic situation? Does he know that he is on the point of losing the life-preserving myth of the inner man which Christianity has treasured up for him? Does he realize what lies in store should this catastrophe ever befall him? Is he even capable of realizing that this would in fact be a catastrophe? And finally, does the individual know that *he* is the makeweight that tips the scales?

587    Happiness and contentment, equability of mind and meaningfulness of life—these can be experienced only by the individual and not by a State, which, on the one hand, is nothing but a convention agreed to by independent individuals and, on the other, continually threatens to paralyse and suppress the individual. The psychiatrist is one of those who know most about the conditions of the soul's welfare, upon which so infinitely much depends in the social sum. The social and political circumstances of the time are certainly of considerable significance, but their importance for the weal or woe of the individual has been boundlessly overestimated in so far as they are taken for the sole deciding factors. In this respect all our social goals commit the error of overlooking the psychology of the

person for whom they are intended and—very often—of promoting only his illusions.

588    I hope, therefore, that a psychiatrist, who in the course of a long life has devoted himself to the causes and consequences of psychic disorders, may be permitted to express his opinion, in all the modesty enjoined upon him as an individual, about the questions raised by the world situation today. I am neither spurred on by excessive optimism nor in love with high ideals, but am merely concerned with the fate of the individual human being—that infinitesimal unit on whom a world depends, and in whom, if we read the meaning of the Christian message aright, even God seeks his goal.

# II

## SYMBOLS AND THE
## INTERPRETATION OF DREAMS

# 1. THE SIGNIFICANCE OF DREAMS

416    Through his language, man tries to designate things in such a way that his words will convey the meaning of what he intends to communicate. But sometimes he uses terms or images that are not strictly descriptive and can be understood only under certain conditions. Take, for instance, the many abbreviations like UN, UNESCO, NATO, etc., which infest our newspapers, or trademarks or the names of patent medicines. Although one cannot see what they mean, they yet have a definite meaning if you know it. Such designations are not *symbols*, they are *signs*. What we call a symbol is a term, a name, or an image which in itself may be familiar to us, but its connotations, use, and application are specific or peculiar and hint at a hidden, vague, or unknown meaning. Take as an example the image of the double adze that occurs frequently on Cretan monuments. We know the object, but we do not know its specific meaning. Again, a Hindu who had been on a visit to England told his friends at home that the English worshipped animals, because he had found eagles, lions, and oxen in their old churches and cathedrals, and he was not aware that these animals were the symbols of the evangelists. There are even many Christians who do not know that they are derived from the vision of Ezekiel, which in turn offers a parallel to the Egyptian Horus and his four sons. Other examples are the wheel and the cross, which are universally known objects, yet under certain conditions they are symbolic and mean something that is still a matter for controversial speculation.

417    A term or image is symbolic when it means more than it denotes or expresses. It has a wider "unconscious" aspect—an aspect that can never be precisely defined or fully explained. This peculiarity is due to the fact that, in exploring the symbol, the mind is finally led towards ideas of a transcendent nature, where

our reason must capitulate. The wheel, for instance, may lead our thoughts to the idea of a "divine" sun, but at this point reason has to admit its inadequacy, for we are unable to define or to establish the existence of a "divine" being. We are merely human, and our intellectual resources are correspondingly limited. We may call something "divine," but this is simply a name, a *façon de parler*, based perhaps on a creed, yet never amounting to a proof.

418 Because there are innumerable things beyond the range of human understanding, we constantly use symbolic expressions and images when referring to them (ecclesiastical language in particular is full of symbols). But this conscious use of symbolism is only one aspect of a psychological fact of great importance: we also produce symbols unconsciously and spontaneously in our dreams.

419 Each act of apperception, or cognition, accomplishes its task only partially; it is never complete. First of all, sense-perception, fundamental to all experience, is restricted by the limited number and quality of our senses, which can however be compensated to a certain extent by the use of instruments, but not sufficiently to eliminate entirely a fringe of uncertainty. Moreover apperception translates the observed fact into a seemingly incommensurable medium—into a psychic event, the nature of which is unknowable. Unknowable, because cognition cannot cognize itself—the psyche cannot know its own psychic substance. There is thus an indefinite number of unknown factors in every experience, in addition to which the object of cognition is always unknown in certain respects since we cannot know the ultimate nature of matter itself.

420 Every conscious act or event thus has an unconscious aspect, just as every sense-perception has a subliminal aspect: for instance, sound below or above audibility, or light below or above visibility. The unconscious part of a psychic event reaches consciousness only indirectly, if at all. The event reveals the existence of its unconscious aspect inasmuch as it is characterized either by emotionality or by a vital importance that has not been realized consciously. The unconscious part is a sort of afterthought, which may become conscious in the course of time by means of intuition or by deeper reflection. But the event can also manifest its unconscious aspect—and this is usually the case

66

—in a dream. The dream shows this aspect in the form of a symbolic image and not as a rational thought. It was the understanding of dreams that first enabled us to investigate the unconscious aspect of conscious psychic events and to discover its nature.

421     It has taken the human mind a long time to arrive at a more or less rational and scientific understanding of the functional meaning of dreams. Freud was the first who tried to elucidate the unconscious background of consciousness in an empirical way. He worked on the general assumption that dream-contents are related to conscious representations through the law of association, i.e., by causal dependence, and are not merely chance occurrences. This assumption is by no means arbitrary but is based on the empirical fact, observed long ago by neurologists and especially by Pierre Janet, that neurotic symptoms are connected with some conscious experience. They even appear to be split-off areas of the conscious mind which, at another time and under different conditions, can be conscious, just as an hysterical anaesthesia can be there one moment and gone the next, only to reappear again after a while. Breuer and Freud recognized more than half a century ago that neurotic symptoms are meaningful and make sense inasmuch as they express a certain thought. In other words, they function in the same manner as dreams: they *symbolize*. A patient, for instance, confronted with an intolerable situation, develops a spasm whenever he tries to swallow: "He can't swallow it." Under similar conditions another patient develops asthma: "He can't breathe the atmosphere at home." A third suffers from a peculiar paralysis of the legs: "He can't go on any more." A fourth vomits everything he eats: "He can't stomach it." And so on. They could all just as well have had dreams of a similar kind.

422     Dreams, of course, display a greater variety and are often full of picturesque and luxuriant fantasy, but they boil down eventually to the same basic thought if one follows Freud's original method of "free association." This method consists in letting the patient go on talking about his dream-images. That is precisely what the non-psychological doctor omits to do. Being always pressed for time, he loathes letting his patient babble on about his fantasies seemingly without end. Yet, if he only knew, his patient is just about to give himself away and to reveal the unconscious background of his ailment. Anyone who talks long

enough will inevitably betray himself by what he says and what he purposely refrains from saying. He may try very hard to lead the doctor and himself away from the real facts, but after a while it is quite easy to see which point he is trying to steer away from. Through apparently rambling and irrational talk, he unconsciously circumscribes a certain area to which he continually returns in ever-renewed attempts to hide it. In his circumlocutions he even makes use of a good deal of symbolism, apparently serving his purpose of hiding and avoiding yet pointing all the time to the core of his predicament.

423    Thus, if the doctor is patient enough, he will hear a wealth of symbolic talk, seemingly calculated to hide something, a secret, from conscious realization. A doctor sees so many things from the seamy side of life that he is seldom far from the truth when he interprets the hints which his patient is emitting as signs of an uneasy conscience. What he eventually discovers, unfortunately, confirms his expectations. Thus far nobody can say anything against Freud's theory of repression and wish-fulfilment as apparent causes of dream symbolism.

424    If one considers the following experience, however, one becomes sceptical. A friend and colleague of mine, travelling for long hours on a train journey through Russia, passed the time by trying to decipher the Cyrillic script of the railway notices in his compartment. He fell into a sort of reverie about what the letters might mean and—following the principle of "free association"—what they reminded him of, and soon he found himself in the midst of all sorts of reminiscences. Among them, to his great displeasure, he did not fail to discover those old and disagreeable companions of sleepless nights, his "complexes"—repressed and carefully avoided topics which the doctor would joyously point to as the most likely causes of a neurosis or the most convincing meaning of a dream.

425    There was no dream, however, merely "free associations" to incomprehensible letters, which means that from any point of the compass you can reach the centre directly. Through free association you arrive at the critical secret thoughts, no matter where you start from, be it symptoms, dreams, fantasies, Cyrillic letters or examples of modern art. At all events, this fact proves nothing with regard to dreams and their real meaning. It only shows the existence of associable material floating about. Very

often dreams have a very definite, as if purposeful, structure, indicating the underlying thought or intention though, as a rule, the latter is not immediately comprehensible.

426 This experience was an eye-opener to me, and, without dismissing the idea of "association" altogether, I thought one should pay more attention to the dream itself, i.e., to its actual form and statement. For instance, a patient of mine dreamed of a drunken, dishevelled, vulgar woman called his "wife" (though in reality his wife was totally different). The dream statement, therefore, is shocking and utterly unlike reality, yet that is what the dream says. Naturally such a statement is not acceptable and is immediately dismissed as dream nonsense. If you let the patient associate freely to the dream, he will most likely try to get away as far as possible from such a shocking thought in order to end up with one of his staple complexes, but you will have learnt nothing about the meaning of this particular dream. What is the unconscious trying to convey by such an obviously untrue statement?

427 If somebody with little experience and knowledge of dreams should think that dreams are just chaotic occurrences without meaning, he is at liberty to do so. But if one assumes that they are normal events, which as a matter of fact they are, one is bound to consider that they are either causal—i.e., that there is a rational cause for their existence—or in some way purposive, or both; in other words, that they make sense.

428 Clearly, the dream is seeking to express the idea of a degenerate female who is closely connected with the dreamer. This idea is projected upon his wife, where the statement becomes untrue. What does it refer to, then?

429 Subtler minds in the Middle Ages already knew that every man "carries Eve, his wife, hidden in his body." [1] It is this feminine element in every man (based on the minority of female genes in his biological make-up) which I have called the *anima*. "She" consists essentially in a certain inferior kind of relatedness to the surroundings and particularly to women, which is kept carefully concealed from others as well as from oneself. A man's visible personality may seem quite normal, while his anima side is sometimes in a deplorable state. This was the case with our

1 [Dominicus Gnosius, *Hermetis Trismegisti Tractatus vere Aureus de Lapide philosophici secreto* (1610), p. 101.—EDITORS.]

dreamer: his female side was not nice. Applied to his anima, the dream-statement hits the nail on the head when it says: you are behaving like a degenerate female. It hits him hard as indeed it should. One should not, however, understand such a dream as evidence for the *moral nature* of the unconscious. It is merely an attempt to balance the lopsidedness of the conscious mind, which had believed the fiction that one was a perfect gentleman throughout.

430 Such experiences taught me to mistrust free association. I no longer followed associations that led far afield and away from the manifest dream-statement. I concentrated rather on the actual dream-text as the thing which was intended by the unconscious, and I began to circumambulate the dream itself, never letting it out of my sight, or as one turns an unknown object round and round in one's hands to absorb every detail of it.

431 But why should one consider dreams, those flimsy, elusive, unreliable, vague, and uncertain phantasms, at all? Are they worthy of our attention? Our rationalism would certainly not recommend them, and the history of dream interpretation before Freud was a sore point anyway; most discouraging in fact, most "unscientific" to say the least of it. *Yet dreams are the commonest and universally accessible source for the investigation of man's symbolizing faculty,* apart from the contents of psychoses, neuroses, myths, and the products of the various arts. All these, however, are more complicated and more difficult to understand, because, when it comes to the question of their individual nature, one cannot venture to interpret such unconscious products without the aid of the originator. Dreams are indeed the chief source of all our knowledge about symbolism.

432 One cannot *invent* symbols; wherever they occur, they have not been devised by conscious intention and wilful selection, because, if such a procedure had been used, they would have been nothing but signs and abbreviations of conscious thoughts. Symbols occur to us spontaneously, as one can see in our dreams, which are not invented but which happen to us. They are not immediately understandable, they need careful analysis by means of association, but, as I have said, not of "free association," which we know always leads back eventually to the emotional thoughts or complexes that are unconsciously captivating our mind. To get there, we have no need of dreams. But in the

early days of medical psychology the general assumption was that dreams were analysed for the purpose of discovering complexes. For this purpose, however, it is sufficient to conduct an association test, which supplies all the necessary hints as I have shown long ago. And not even this test is necessary, because one can obtain the same result by letting people talk long enough.

433    There can be no doubt that dreams often arise from an emotional disturbance in which the habitual complexes are involved. The habitual complexes are the tender spots of the psyche, which react most quickly to a problematical external situation. But I began to suspect that dreams might have another, more interesting function. The fact that they eventually lead back to the complexes is not the specific merit of dreams. If we want to learn what a dream means and what specific function it fulfils, we must disregard its inevitable outcome, the complex. We must put a check on limitless "free" association, a restriction provided by the dream itself. By free association, we move away from the individual dream-image and lose sight of it. We must, on the contrary, keep close to the dream and its individual form. The dream is its own limitation. It is itself the criterion of what belongs to it and of what leads away from it. All material that does not lie within the scope of the dream, or that oversteps the boundaries set by its individual form, leads astray and produces nothing but the complexes, and we do not know whether they belong to the dream or not since they can be produced in so many other ways. There is, for instance, an almost infinite variety of images by which the sexual act can be "symbolized," or rather allegorized. But the dream obviously intends its own specific expression in spite of the fact that the resultant associations will lead to the idea of sexual intercourse. This is no news and is easy to see, but the real task is to understand why the dream has chosen its own individual expression.

434    Only the material that is clearly and visibly indicated as belonging to the dream by the dream-images themselves should be used for interpretation. While free association moves away from the theme of the dream in something like a zigzag line, the new method, as I have always said, is more like a circumambulation, the centre of which is the dream-image. One concentrates on the specific topics, on the dream itself, and disregards the frequent attempts of the dreamer to break away from it. This ever-

present "neurotic" dissociative tendency has many aspects, but at bottom it seems to consist in a basic resistance of the conscious mind to anything unconscious and unknown. As we know, this often fierce resistance is typical of the psychology of primitive societies, which are as a rule conservative and show pronounced misoneistic tendencies. Anything new and unknown causes distinct and even superstitious fear. The primitive manifests all the reactions of a wild animal to untoward events. Our highly differentiated civilization is not at all free from such primitive behaviour. A new idea that is not exactly in line with general expectations meets with the severest obstacles of a psychological kind. It is given no credit, but is feared, combatted, and abhorred in every way. Many pioneers can tell a story of misery, all due to the primitive misoneism of their contemporaries. When it comes to psychology, one of the youngest of the sciences, you can see misoneism at work, and in dealing with your own dreams you can easily observe your reactions when you have to admit a disagreeable thought. It is chiefly and above all fear of the unexpected and unknown that makes people eager to use free association as a means of escape. I do not know how many times in my professional work I have had to repeat the words: "Now let's get back to your dream. What does the *dream* say?"

435    If one wants to understand a dream it must be taken seriously, and one must also assume that it means what it manifestly says, since there is no valid reason to suppose that it is anything other than it is. Yet the apparent futility of dreams is so overwhelming that not only the dreamer but the interpreter as well may easily succumb to the prejudice of the "nothing but" explanation. Whenever a dream gets difficult and obstinate, the temptation to dismiss it altogether is not far away.

436    When I was doing fieldwork with a primitive tribe in East Africa, I discovered to my amazement that they denied having dreams at all. But by patient indirect talk I soon found that they had dreams all right, like everybody else, but were convinced that their dreams meant nothing. "Dreams of ordinary men mean nothing," they said. The only dreams that mattered were those of the chief and the medicine-man, which concerned the welfare of the tribe. Such dreams were highly appreciated. The only drawback was that the chief as well as the medicine-man denied having any more dreams "since the British were in the

country." The District Commissioner had taken over the function of the "big dream."

437     This incident shows that even in a primitive society opinions about dreams are ambivalent, just as in our society, where most people see nothing in dreams while a minority thinks very highly of them. The Church, for instance, has long known of *somnia a Deo missa* (dreams sent by God), and in our own time we have watched the growth of a scientific discipline which aims at exploring the vast field of unconscious processes. Yet the average man thinks little or nothing about dreams, and even a thoroughly educated person shares the common ignorance and underrates everything remotely connected with the "unconscious."

438     The very existence of an unconscious psyche is denied by a great number of scientists and philosophers, who often use the naïve argument that if there were an unconscious psyche there would be two subjects in the individual instead of one. But that is precisely the case, in spite of the supposed unity of the personality. It is, indeed, the great trouble of our time that so many people exist whose right hand does not know what their left is doing. It is by no means the neurotic alone who finds himself in this predicament. It is not a recent development, nor can it be blamed on Christian morality; it is, on the contrary, the symptom of a general unconsciousness that is the heritage of all mankind.

439     The development of consciousness is a slow and laborious process that took untold ages to reach the civilized state (which we date somewhat arbitrarily from the invention of writing, about 4000 B.C.). Although the development since that date seems to be considerable, it is still far from complete. Indefinitely large areas of the mind still remain in darkness. What we call "psyche" is by no means identical with consciousness and its contents. Those who deny the existence of the unconscious do not realize that they are actually assuming our knowledge of the psyche to be complete, with nothing left for further discoveries. It is exactly as if they declared our present knowledge of nature to be the summit of all possible knowledge. Our psyche is part of nature, and its enigma is just as limitless. We cannot define "nature" or "psyche," but can only state what, at present, we understand them to be. No man in his senses, therefore, could make

such a statement as "there is no unconscious," i.e., no psychic contents of which he and others are unconscious—not to mention the mountain of convincing evidence that medical science has accumulated. It is not, of course, scientific responsibility or honesty that causes such resistance, but age-old misoneism, fear of the new and unknown.

440     This peculiar resistance to the unknown part of the psyche has its historical reasons. Consciousness is a very recent acquisition and as such is still in an "experimental state"—frail, menaced by specific dangers, and easily injured. As a matter of fact one of the most common mental derangements among primitives consists in the "loss of a soul," which, as the term indicates, means a noticeable dissociation of consciousness. On the primitive level the psyche or soul is by no means a unit, as is widely supposed. Many primitives assume that, as well as his own, a man has a "bush-soul," incarnate in a wild animal or a tree, with which he is connected by a kind of psychic identity. This is what Lévy-Bruhl called *participation mystique*.[2] In the case of an animal it is a sort of brother, so much so that a man whose brother is a crocodile is supposed to be safe while swimming across a crocodile-infested river. In the case of a tree, the tree is supposed to have authority over the individual like a parent. Injury to the bush-soul means an equal injury to the man. Others assume that a man has a number of souls, which shows clearly that the primitive often feels that he consists of several units. This indicates that his psyche is far from being safely synthesized; on the contrary, it threatens to fall asunder only too easily under the onslaught of unchecked emotions.

441     What we observe in the seemingly remote sphere of the primitive mind has by no means vanished in our advanced civilization. Only too often, as I have said, the right hand does not know what the left is doing, and in a state of violent affect one frequently forgets who one is, so that people can ask: "What the devil has got into you?" We are possessed and altered by our moods, we can suddenly be unreasonable, or important facts unaccountably vanish from our memory. We talk about being able to "control ourselves," but self-control is a rare and remarkable

[2] Lévy-Bruhl later retracted this term under the pressure of adverse criticism, to which he unfortunately succumbed. His critics were wrong inasmuch as unconscious identity is a well-known psychological fact.

virtue. If you ask your friends or relatives they may be able to tell you things about yourself of which you have no knowledge. One almost always forgets or omits to apply to oneself the criticism that one hands out so freely to others, fascinated by the mote in one's brother's eye.

442     All these well-known facts show beyond a doubt that, on the heights of our civilization, human consciousness has not yet attained a reasonable degree of continuity. It is still dissociable and vulnerable, in a way fortunately so, since the dissociability of the psyche is also an advantage in that it enables us to concentrate on one point by dismissing everything else that might claim attention. It makes a great difference, however, whether your consciousness purposely splits off and suppresses a part of the psyche temporarily, or whether the same thing *happens* to you, so that the psyche splits spontaneously without your consent and knowledge, or perhaps even against your will. The first is a civilized achievement, the second a primitive and archaic condition or a pathological event and the cause of a neurosis. It is the "loss of a soul," the symptom of a still existing mental primitivity.

443     It is a long way indeed from primitivity to a reliable cohesion of consciousness. Even in our days the unity of consciousness is a doubtful affair, since only a little affect is needed to disrupt its continuity. On the other hand the perfect control of emotion, however desirable from one point of view, would be a questionable accomplishment, for it would deprive social intercourse of all variety, colour, warmth, and charm.

75

## 2. THE FUNCTIONS OF THE UNCONSCIOUS

444    Our new method treats the dream as a spontaneous product
of the psyche about which there is no previous assumption except that it somehow makes sense. This is no more than every
science assumes, namely that its object is worthy of investigation. No matter how low one's opinion of the unconscious may
be, the unconscious is at least on a level with the louse, which,
after all, enjoys the honest interest of the entomologist. As to the
alleged boldness of the hypothesis that an unconscious psyche
exists, I must emphasize that a more modest formulation could
hardly be imagined. It is so simple that it amounts to a tautol-
ogy: a content of consciousness disappears and cannot be reproduced. The best we can say of it is: the thought (or whatever it
was) has become unconscious, or is cut off from consciousness, so
that it cannot even be remembered. Or else it may happen that
we have an inkling or hunch of something which is about to
break into consciousness: "something is in the air," "we smell a
rat," and so on. To speak under these conditions of latent or
unconscious contents is hardly a daring hypothesis.

445    When something vanishes from consciousness it does not dissolve into thin air or cease to exist, any more than a car disap-
pearing round a corner becomes non-existent. It is simply out
of sight, and, as we may meet the car again, so we may come
across a thought again which was previously lost. We find the
same thing with sensation, as the following experiment proves.
If you produce a continuous note on the edge of audibility, you
will observe in listening to it that at regular intervals it is au-
dible and inaudible. These oscillations are due to a periodic increase and decrease of attention. The note never ceases to exist
with static intensity. It is merely the decrease of attention that
causes its apparent disappearance.

446    The unconscious, therefore, consists in the first place of a

multitude of temporarily eclipsed contents which, as experience shows, continue to influence the conscious processes. A man in a distracted state of mind goes to a certain place in his room, obviously to fetch something. Then he suddenly stops perplexed: he has forgotten why he got up and what he was after. He gropes absent-mindedly among a whole collection of objects, completely at sea as to what he wants to find. Suddenly he wakes up, having discovered the thing he wants. He behaves like a man walking in his sleep oblivious of his original purpose, yet unconsciously guided by it. If you observe the behaviour of a neurotic, you can see him performing apparently conscious and purposeful acts yet, when you ask him about them, you discover to your surprise that he is either unconscious of them or has something quite different in mind. He hears and does not hear, he sees yet is blind, he knows and does not know at the same time. Thousands of such observations have convinced the specialist that unconscious contents behave as if they were conscious, and that you can never be sure whether thought, speech, or action is conscious or not. Something so obvious to yourself that you cannot imagine it to be invisible to anybody can be as good as nonexistent to your fellows, and yet they behave as if they were just as conscious of it as you are yourself.

447    This kind of behaviour has given rise to the medical prejudice that hysterical patients are confirmed liars. Yet the surplus of lies they seem to produce is due to the uncertainty of their mental state, to the dissociability of their consciousness, which is liable to unpredictable eclipses, just as their skin shows unexpected and changing areas of anaesthesia. There is no certainty whether a needle-prick will be registered or not. If their attention can be focused on a certain point, the whole surface of their body may be completely anaesthetized, and, when attention relaxes, sense-perception is instantly restored. Moreover when one hypnotizes such cases one can easily demonstrate that they are aware of everything that has been done in an anaesthetized area or during an eclipse of consciousness. They can remember every detail just as if they had been fully conscious during the experiment. I recall a similar case of a woman who was admitted to the clinic in a state of complete stupor. Next day when she came to, she knew who she was, but did not know where she was nor how or why she had come there, nor did she know the date. I hypno-

tized her, and she could tell me a verifiable story of why she fell ill, how she had got to the clinic, and who had received her, with all the details. As there was a clock in the entrance hall, though not in a very conspicuous place, she could also remember the time of her admission to the minute. Everything happened as if she had been in a completely normal condition and not deeply unconscious.

448   It is true that the bulk of our evidential material comes from clinical observation. That is the reason why many critics assume that the unconscious and its manifestations belong to the sphere of psychopathology as neurotic or psychotic symptoms and that they do not occur in a normal mental state. But, as has been pointed out long ago, neurotic phenomena are not by any means the exclusive products of disease. They are as a matter of fact *normal occurrences pathologically exaggerated,* and therefore just more obvious than their normal parallels. One can indeed observe all hysterical symptoms in a diminutive form in normal individuals, but they are so slight that they usually pass unnoticed. In this respect, everyday life is a mine of evidential material.

449   Just as conscious contents can vanish into the unconscious, other contents can also arise from it. Besides a majority of mere recollections, really new thoughts and creative ideas can appear which have never been conscious before. They grow up from the dark depths like a lotus, and they form an important part of the subliminal psyche. This aspect of the unconscious is of particular relevance in dealing with dreams. One must always bear in mind that dream material does not necessarily consist of memories; it may just as well contain new thoughts that are not yet conscious.

450   Forgetting is a normal process, in which certain conscious contents lose their specific energy through a deflection of attention. When interest turns elsewhere, it leaves former contents in the shadow, just as a searchlight illuminates a new area by leaving another to disappear in the darkness. This is unavoidable, for consciousness can keep only a few images in full clarity at one time, and even this clarity fluctuates, as I have mentioned. "Forgetting" may be defined as temporarily subliminal contents remaining outside the range of vision against one's will. But the forgotten contents have not ceased to exist. Although they cannot be reproduced they are present in a subliminal state, from

which they can rise up spontaneously at any time, often after many years of apparently total oblivion, or they can be fetched back by hypnosis.

451 Besides normal forgetting, there are the cases described by Freud of disagreeable memories which one is only too ready to lose. As Nietzsche has remarked, when pride is insistent enough, memory prefers to give way. Thus among the lost memories we encounter not a few that owe their subliminal state (and their incapacity to be reproduced at will) to their disagreeable and incompatible nature. These are the *repressed* contents.

452 As a parallel to normal forgetting, *subliminal sense-perceptions* should be mentioned, because they play a not unimportant role in our daily life. We see, hear, smell and taste many things without noticing them at the time, either because our attention is deflected or because the stimulus is too slight to produce a conscious impression. But in spite of their apparent non-existence they can influence consciousness. A well-known example is the case of the professor walking in the country with a pupil, deep in serious conversation. Suddenly he notices that his thoughts are interrupted by an unexpected flow of memories from his early childhood. He cannot account for it, as he is unable to discover any associative connection with the subject of his conversation. He stops and looks back: there at a little distance is a farm, through which they had passed a short while ago, and he remembers that soon afterwards images of his childhood began to surge up. "Let us go back to the farm," he says to his pupil; "it must be about there that my fantasies started." Back at the farm, the professor notices the smell of geese. Instantly he recognizes it as the cause of the interruption: in his early youth he had lived on a farm where there were geese, whose characteristic smell had formed a lasting impression and caused the reproduction of the memory-images. He had noticed the smell while passing the farmyard, subliminally, and the unconscious perception had called back long-forgotten memories.

453 This example illustrates how the subliminal perception released early childhood memories, the energic tension of which proved to be strong enough to interrupt the conversation. The perception was subliminal because the attention was engaged elsewhere, and the stimulus was not strong enough to deflect it and to reach consciousness directly. Such phenomena are frequent in everyday life, but mostly they pass unnoticed.

454    A relatively rare but all the more astonishing phenomenon
that falls into the same category is *cryptomnesia*, or the "concealed recollection." It consists in the fact that suddenly, mostly
in the flow of creative writing, a word, a sentence, an image, a
metaphor, or even a whole story appears which may exhibit a
strange or otherwise remarkable character. If you ask the author
where this fragment comes from, he does not know, and it becomes obvious that he has not even noticed it as anything peculiar. I will quote one such example from Nietzsche's *Thus Spake
Zarathustra*. The author describes Zarathustra's "descent to
hell" with certain characteristic details which coincide almost
word for word with the narration in a ship's log from the year
1686.

455    Nietzsche, *Thus Spake Zarathustra* (1883) [1]

Now about the time that Zarathustra sojourned on the Happy
Isles, it happened that a ship
anchored at the isle on which
the smoking mountain stands,
and the crew went ashore to
shoot rabbits. About the noon-
tide hour, however, when the
captain and his men were together again, they suddenly saw
a man coming towards them
through the air, and a voice said
distinctly: "It is time! It is highest time!" But when the figure
drew close to them, flying past
quickly like a shadow in the
direction of the volcano, they
recognized with the greatest dismay that it was Zarathustra.
. . . "Behold," said the old
helmsman, "Zarathustra goes
down to hell!"

Justinus Kerner, *Blätter aus
Prevorst* (1831-39) [2]

The four captains and a mer-
chant, Mr. Bell, went ashore on
the island of Mount Stromboli
to shoot rabbits. At three o'clock
they mustered the crew to go
aboard, when, to their inexpress-
ible astonishment, they saw two
men flying rapidly towards them
through the air. One was dressed
in black, the other in grey. They
came past them very closely, in
the greatest haste, and to their
utmost dismay descended into
the crater of the terrible volcano, Mount Stromboli. They
recognized the pair as acquaintances from London.

[1] Ch. XL, "Great Events" (trans. Common, p. 180, slightly modified). [For other
discussions, see *Psychiatric Studies*, pars. 140ff. and 180ff.—EDITORS.]
[2] Vol. IV, p. 57, headed "An Extract of Awe-Inspiring Import from the Log of
the Ship *Sphinx* in the Year 1686, in the Mediterranean."

456    When I read Nietzsche's story I was struck by its peculiar style, which is different from Nietzsche's usual language, and by the strange images of a ship anchored off a mythological island, of a captain and his crew shooting rabbits, and of the descent to hell of a man who was recognized as an old acquaintance. The parallels with Kerner could not be a mere coincidence. Kerner's collection dates from about 1835 and is probably the only extant source of the seaman's yarn. At least I was certain that Nietzsche must have gleaned it from there. He retells the story with a few significant variations and as if it were his own invention. As it was in the year 1902 that I came across this case, I still had the opportunity to write to Elizabeth Förster-Nietzsche, the author's sister, and she remembered that she and her brother had read the *Blätter aus Prevorst* when Nietzsche was eleven years old, though she did not remember this particular story. The reason why I remembered it was that I had come across Kerner's collection four years before, in a private library; and, as I was interested in the writings of the physicians of that time as the forerunners of medical psychology, I had read through all the volumes of the *Blätter*. Naturally I should have forgotten the yarn in the course of time, because it did not interest me in any way. But in reading Nietzsche I suddenly had a *sentiment du déjà vu*, followed by a dim recollection of old-fashioned cut, and gradually the picture of Kerner's book filtered into my consciousness.

457    Benoît, who produced a surprising parallel to Rider Haggard's *She* in his novel *L'Atlantide*, when accused of plagiarism had to answer that he had never come across Rider Haggard's book and was entirely unaware of its existence. This case could also have been one of cryptomnesia, if it had not been an elaboration of a sort of *représentation collective*, as Lévy-Bruhl has named certain general ideas characteristic of primitive societies. I shall be dealing with these later on.

458    What I have said about the unconscious will give the reader a fair idea of the subliminal material on which the spontaneous production of dream-symbols is based. It is evidently material that owes its unconsciousness chiefly to the fact that certain conscious contents must necessarily lose their energy, i.e., the attention bestowed on them, or their specific emotional tone, in order to make room for new contents. If they were to retain their en-

ergy, they would remain above the threshold and one could not get rid of them. It is as if consciousness were a sort of projector that casts its light (of attention or interest) on new perceptions —due to arrive presently—as well as on the traces of former ones in a dormant state. As a conscious act, this process can be understood as an intentional and voluntary event. Yet just as often consciousness is forced to turn on its light by the intensity of an external or internal stimulus.

459     This observation is not superfluous, for there are many people who overestimate the role of will-power and think nothing can happen in their minds that they do not intend. But, for the sake of psychological understanding, one should learn to discriminate carefully between *intentional and unintentional contents*. The former are derived from the ego-personality, while the latter arise from a source which is not identical with the ego, that is, from a subliminal part of the ego, from its "other side," which is in a way another subject. The existence of this other subject is by no means a pathological symptom, but a normal fact that can be observed at any time anywhere.

460     I once had a discussion with one of my colleagues about another doctor who had done something I had qualified as "utterly idiotic." This doctor was my colleague's personal friend, and moreover a believer in the somewhat fanatical creed to which my colleague subscribed. Both were teetotalers. He impulsively replied to my criticism: "Of course he is an ass"—pulling himself up short—"a highly intelligent man, I meant to say." I mildly remarked that the ass came first, whereupon he angrily denied ever having said such a thing about his friend, and to an unbeliever at that. This man was highly regarded as a scientist, but his right hand did not know what his left was doing. Such people are not fit for psychology and, as a matter of fact, do not like it. But that is the way the voice from the other side is usually treated: "I didn't mean it, I never said so." And in the end, as Nietzsche says, memory prefers to give way.

## 3. THE LANGUAGE OF DREAMS

461     All contents of consciousness have been or can become subliminal, thus forming part of the psychic sphere which we call
the unconscious. All urges, impulses, intentions, affects, all perceptions and intuitions, all rational and irrational thoughts,
conclusions, inductions, deductions, premises, etc., as well as all
categories of feeling, have their subliminal equivalents, which
may be subject to partial, temporary, or chronic unconsciousness. One uses a word or a concept, for instance, that in another
connection has an entirely different meaning of which one is
momentarily unconscious, and this can lead to a ridiculous or
even disastrous misunderstanding. Even a most carefully defined
philosophical or mathematical concept, which we are sure does
not contain more than we have put into it, is nevertheless more
than we assume. It is at the least a psychic event, the nature of
which is actually unknowable. The very numbers you use in
counting are more than you take them for. They are at the same
time mythological entities (for the Pythagoreans they were even
divine), but you are certainly unaware of this when you use
numbers for a practical purpose.

462     We are also unconscious of the fact that general terms like
"state," "money," "health," "society" etc. usually mean more
than they are supposed to signify. They are general only because
we assume them to be so, but in practical reality they have all
sorts of nuances of meaning. I am not thinking of the deliberate
twisting of such concepts in their Communist usage, but of the
fact that even when they are understood in their proper sense
they nevertheless vary slightly from person to person. The reason for this variation is that a general notion is received into an
individual context and is therefore understood and used in an
individual way. As long as concepts are identical with mere
words, the variation is almost imperceptible and of no practical

83

importance. But when an exact definition or a careful explanation is needed, one can occasionally discover the most amazing variations, not only in the purely intellectual understanding of the term, but particularly in its emotional tone and its application. As a rule these variations are subliminal and therefore never realized.

463 One may dismiss such differences as redundant or over-nice distinctions, but the fact that they exist shows that even the most banal contents of consciousness have a penumbra of uncertainty around them, which justifies us in thinking that each of them carries a definite subliminal charge. Although this aspect plays little role in everyday life, one must bear it in mind when analysing dreams. I recall a dream of my own that baffled me for a while. In this dream, a certain Mr. X was desperately trying to get behind me and jump on my back. I knew nothing of this gentleman except that he had succeeded in twisting something I had said into a rather grotesque travesty of my meaning. This kind of thing had frequently happened to me in my professional life, and I had never bothered to realize whether it made me angry or not. But as it is of practical importance to maintain conscious control of one's emotions, the dream pointedly brought up the incident again in the apparent "disguise" of a colloquialism. This saying, common enough in ordinary speech, is "Du kannst mir auf den Buckel steigen" (you can climb on my back), which means "I don't give a damn what you say."

464 One could say that this dream-image was symbolic, for it did not state the situation directly but in a roundabout way, through a concretized colloquial metaphor which I did not understand at first sight. Since I have no reason to believe that the unconscious has any intention of concealing things, I must be careful not to project such a device on its activity. It is characteristic of dreams to prefer pictorial and picturesque language to colourless and merely rational statements. This is certainly not an intentional concealment; it simply emphasizes our inability to understand the emotionally charged picture-language of dreams.

465 As daily adaptation to the reality of things demands accurate statements, we have learnt to discard the trimming of fantasy, and have thus lost a quality that is still characteristic of the primitive mind. Primitive thinking sees its object surrounded

by a fringe of associations which have become more or less unconscious in civilized man. Thus animals, plants, and inanimate objects can acquire properties that are most unexpected to the white man. A nocturnal animal seen by day is, for the primitive, quite obviously a medicine-man who has temporarily changed his shape; or else it is a doctor-animal or an animal-ancestor, or somebody's bush-soul. A tree can be part of a man's life, it has a soul and a voice, and the man shares its fate, and so on. Certain South American Indians assure you that they are red *araras* (parrots), although they are quite aware that they have no feathers and don't look like birds. In the primitive's world, things do not have the same sharp boundaries they do in ours. What we call psychic identity or *participation mystique* has been stripped off our world of things. It is exactly this halo, or "fringe of consciousness," as William James calls it, which gives a colourful and fantastic aspect to the primitive's world. We have lost it to such a degree that we do not recognize it when we meet it again, and are baffled by its incomprehensibility. With us such things are kept below the threshold; and when they occasionally reappear, we are convinced that something is wrong.

466    I have more than once been consulted by highly educated and otherwise intelligent people because they had peculiar dreams, involuntary fantasies, or even visions, which shocked or frightened them. They assumed that nobody in a sound mental condition could suffer from such phenomena, and that a person who had a vision was certainly pathological. A theologian I knew once avowed his belief that Ezekiel's visions were morbid symptoms, and that when Moses and other prophets heard "voices" they were suffering from hallucinations. Naturally he got into a panic when some spontaneous events of this kind happened to him. We are so used to the rational surface of our world that we cannot imagine anything untoward happening within the confines of common sense. If our mind once in a while does something thoroughly unexpected, we are terrified and immediately think of a pathological disturbance, whereas primitive man would think of fetishes, spirits, or gods but would never doubt his sanity. Modern man is very much in the situation of the old doctor who was himself a psychotic patient. When I asked him how he was, he replied that he had had a wonderful night disinfecting the whole heaven with chloride of

mercury but had found no trace of God. What we find instead of God is a neurosis or something worse, and the fear of God has changed into a phobia or anxiety neurosis. The emotion remains the same, only its object has changed its name and nature for the worse.

467    I remember a professor of philosophy and psychology who consulted me about his cancer phobia. He suffered from a compulsive conviction that he had a malignant tumour, although nothing of the sort was ever found in dozens of X-ray pictures. "Oh, I know there is nothing," he would say, "but there still *might* be something." Such a confession is certainly far more humiliating to a strong intellect than the belief of a primitive that he is plagued by a ghost. Malevolent spirits are at least a perfectly admissible hypothesis in a primitive society, but it is a shattering experience for a civilized person to have to admit that he is the victim of nothing more than a foolish prank of the imagination. The primitive phenomenon of obsession has not vanished, it is the same as ever. It is only interpreted in a different and more obnoxious way.

468    Many dreams present images and associations that are analogous to primitive ideas, myths, and rites. These dream-images were called "archaic remnants" by Freud. The term suggests that they are psychic elements left over from times long ago and still adhering to our modern mind. This point of view forms part of the prevailing depreciation of the unconscious as a mere appendix of consciousness or, to put it more drastically, a dustbin which collects all the refuse of the conscious mind—all things discarded, disused, worthless, forgotten, and repressed.

469    This opinion had to be abandoned in more recent times, since further investigation has shown that such images and associations belong to the regular structure of the unconscious and can be observed more or less everywhere, in the dreams of highly educated as well as illiterate people, of the intelligent as well as the stupid. They are in no sense dead or meaningless "remnants"; on the contrary, they still continue to function and are therefore of vital value just because of their "historical" nature. They are a sort of language that acts as a bridge between the way in which we consciously express our thoughts and a more primitive, more colourful and pictorial form of expression—a language that appeals directly to feeling and emotion. Such a lan-

guage is needed to translate certain truths from their "cultural" form (where they are utterly ineffectual) into a form that hits the nail on the head. For instance, there is a lady well known for her stupid prejudices and stubborn arguments. The doctor tries in vain to instil some insight. He says: "My dear lady, your views are indeed very interesting and original. But you see, there are many people who unfortunately lack your assumptions and have need of your forbearance. Couldn't you . . ." etc. He could just as well talk to a stone. But the dream follows a different method. She dreams: there is a great social affair to which she is invited. She is received by her hostess (a very bright woman) at the door with the words: "Oh, how nice that you have come, all your friends are already here and are expecting you." She leads her to a door, opens it, and the lady steps into—a cowshed.

470    This is a more concrete and drastic language, simple enough to be understood even by a blockhead. Although the lady would not admit the point of the dream, it nevertheless went home, and after a time she was forced to accept it because she could not help seeing the self-inflicted joke.

471    The message of the unconscious is of greater importance than most people realize. As consciousness is exposed to all sorts of external attractions and distractions, it is easily led astray and seduced into following ways that are unsuited to its individuality. The general function of dreams is to balance such disturbances in the mental equilibrium by producing contents of a complementary or compensatory kind. Dreams of high vertiginous places, balloons, aeroplanes, flying and falling, often accompany states of consciousness characterized by fictitious assumptions, overestimation of oneself, unrealistic opinions, and grandiose plans. If the warning of the dream is not heeded, real accidents take its place. One stumbles, falls downstairs, runs into a car, etc. I remember the case of a man who was inextricably involved in a number of shady affairs. He developed an almost morbid passion for dangerous mountain-climbing as a sort of compensation: he was trying to "get above himself." In one dream he saw himself stepping off the summit of a high mountain into the air. When he told me his dream, I instantly saw the risk he was running, and I tried my best to emphasize the warning and convince him of the need to restrain himself. I even told him that the dream meant his death in a mountain accident. It

was in vain. Six months later he "stepped off into the air." A mountain guide watched him and a young friend letting themselves down on a rope in a difficult place. The friend had found a temporary foothold on a ledge, and the dreamer was following him down. Suddenly he let go of the rope "as if he were jumping into the air," as the guide reported afterwards. He fell on his friend, and both went down and were killed.

472    Another typical case was that of a lady who was living above herself in a fantasy of distinction and austerity. But she had shocking dreams, reminding her of all sorts of unsavoury things. When I put my finger on them, she indignantly refused to acknowledge them. The dreams then became menacing, full of references to the long lonely walks she took in the woods near the town, where she indulged in soulful musings. I saw the danger and warned her insistently, but she would not listen. A week later a sexual pervert attacked her murderously, and only in the nick of time was she rescued by some people who had heard her screams. Obviously she had a secret longing for some such adventure and preferred to pay the price of two broken ribs and the fracture of a laryngeal cartilage, just as the mountain climber at least had the satisfaction of finding a definite way out of his predicament.

473    Dreams prepare, announce, or warn about certain situations, often long before they actually happen. This is not necessarily a miracle or a precognition. Most crises or dangerous situations have a long incubation, only the conscious mind is not aware of it. Dreams can betray the secret. They often do, but just as often, it seems, they do not. Therefore our assumption of a benevolent hand restraining us in time is doubtful. Or, to put it more positively, it seems that a benevolent agency is at work sometimes but at other times not. The mysterious finger may even point the way to perdition. One cannot afford to be naïve in dealing with dreams. They originate in a spirit that is not quite human, but is rather the breath of nature—of the beautiful and generous as well as the cruel goddess. If we want to characterize this spirit, we would do better to turn to the ancient mythologies and the fables of the primeval forest. Civilization is a most expensive process and its acquisitions have been paid for by enormous losses, the extent of which we have largely forgotten or have never appreciated.

474    Through our efforts to understand dreams we become acquainted with what William James has aptly called the "fringe of consciousness." What appear to be redundant and unwelcome accessories are, if studied more closely, the almost invisible roots of conscious contents, i.e., their subliminal aspects. They form the psychic material that must be considered as the intermediary between unconscious and conscious contents, or the bridge that spans the gap between consciousness and the ultimately physiological foundations of the psyche. The practical importance of such a bridge can hardly be overrated. It is the indispensable link between the rational world of consciousness and the world of instinct. The more our consciousness is influenced by prejudices, fantasies, infantile wishes, and the lure of external objects, the more the already existing gap will widen out into a neurotic dissociation and lead to an artificial life far removed from healthy instincts, nature, and truth. Dreams try to re-establish the equilibrium by restoring the images and emotions that express the state of the unconscious. One can hardly ever restore the original condition by rational talk, which is far too flat and colourless. But, as my examples have shown, the language of dreams provides just those images which appeal to the deeper strata of the psyche. One could even say that the interpretation of dreams enriches consciousness to such an extent that it relearns the forgotten language of the instincts.

475    In so far as instincts are physiological urges, they are perceived by the senses and at the same time manifest themselves as fantasies. But in so far as they are not perceived sensually, they reveal their presence only in images. The vast majority of instinctive phenomena consists, however, of images, many of which are of a symbolic nature whose meaning is not immediately recognizable. One finds them chiefly in that twilight realm between dim consciousness and the unconscious background of the dream. Sometimes a dream is of such vital importance that its message reaches consciousness no matter how uncomfortable or shocking it may be. From the standpoint of mental equilibrium and physiological health in general, it is much better for the conscious and the unconscious to be connected and to move on parallel lines than for them to be dissociated. In this respect the production of symbols can be considered a most valuable function.

476    One will naturally ask what is the point of this function if its symbols should pass unnoticed or prove to be incomprehensible? But lack of conscious understanding does not mean that the dream has no effect at all. Even civilized man can occasionally observe that a dream which he cannot remember can slightly alter his mood for better or worse. Dreams can be "understood" to a certain extent in a subliminal way, and that is mostly how they work. Only when a dream is very impressive, or repeats itself often, do interpretation and conscious understanding become desirable. But in pathological cases an interpretation is imperative and should be undertaken if there are no counter-indications, such as the existence of a latent psychosis, which is, as it were, only waiting for a suitable releasing agent to burst forth in full force. Unintelligent and incompetent application of dream analysis and interpretation is indeed not advisable, and particularly not when there is a dissociation between a very one-sided consciousness and a correspondingly irrational or "crazy" unconscious.

477    Owing to the infinite variety of conscious contents and their deviation from the ideal middle line, the unconscious compensation is equally varied, so that one would be hard put to it to say whether dreams and their symbols are classifiable or not. Though there are dreams and occasional symbols—better called motifs in this case—which are typical and occur often, most dreams are individual and atypical. Typical motifs are falling, flying, being chased by dangerous animals or men, being insufficiently or absurdly clothed in public places, being in a hurry or lost in a milling crowd, fighting with useless weapons or being utterly defenceless, running and getting nowhere, and so on. A typical infantile motif is the dream of growing infinitely small or infinitely big, or of being transformed from the one into the other.

478    A noteworthy phenomenon is the recurrent dream. There are cases of dreams repeating themselves from the days of childhood to the advanced years of adult life. Such dreams usually compensate a defect in one's conscious attitude, or they date from a traumatic moment that has left behind some specific prejudice, or they anticipate a future event of some importance. I myself dreamt of a motif that was repeated many times over a period of years. It was that I discovered a part of a wing of my

house which I did not know existed. Sometimes it was the place where my parents lived—who had died long ago—where my father, to my great surprise, had a laboratory in which he studied the comparative anatomy of fishes, and where my mother ran a hostelry for ghostly visitors. Usually the wing or independent guest-house was an historical building several hundred years old, long forgotten, yet my ancestral property. It contained interesting old furniture, and towards the end of this series of recurrent dreams I discovered an old library whose books were unknown to me. Finally, in the last dream, I opened one of the old volumes and found in it a profusion of the most marvellous symbolic pictures. When I awoke, my heart was pounding with excitement.

479    Some time before this dream I had placed an order with an antiquarian bookseller abroad for one of the Latin alchemical classics, because I had come across a quotation that I thought might be connected with early Byzantine alchemy, and I wished to verify it. Several weeks after my dream a parcel arrived containing a parchment volume of the sixteenth century with many most fascinating symbolic pictures. They instantly reminded me of my dream library. As the rediscovery of alchemy forms an important part of my life as a pioneer of psychology, the motif of the unknown annex of my house can easily be understood as an anticipation of a new field of interest and research. At all events, from that moment thirty years ago the recurrent dream came to an end.

480    Symbols, like dreams, are natural products, but they do not occur only in dreams. They can appear in any number of psychic manifestations: there are symbolic thoughts and feelings, symbolic acts and situations, and it often looks as if not only the unconscious but even inanimate objects were concurring in the arrangement of symbolic patterns. There are numerous well-authenticated stories of a clock that stopped at the moment of its owner's death, like Frederick the Great's pendulum clock at Sans Souci; of a mirror that broke, or a boiling coffee-pot that exploded, just before or during a crisis; and so on. Even if the sceptic refuses to credit such reports, stories of this kind are ever renewed and are told again and again, which is ample proof of their psychological importance, even though ignorant people deny their factual existence.

481　　The most important symbols, however, are not individual but collective in their nature and origin. They are found principally in the religions. The believer assumes that they are of divine origin—that they are revealed. The sceptic thinks they are invented. Both are wrong. It is true that, on the one hand, such symbols have for centuries been the objects of careful and quite conscious elaboration and differentiation, as in the case of dogmas. But, on the other hand, they are *représentations collectives* dating from dim and remote ages, and these are "revelations" only in the sense that they are images originating in dreams and creative fantasies. The latter are involuntary, spontaneous manifestations and by no means arbitrary and intentional inventions.

482　　There was never a genius who sat down with his pen or brush and said: "Now I am going to invent a symbol." No one can take a more or less rational thought, reached as a logical conclusion or deliberately chosen, and then disguise it as a "symbolic" phantasmagoria. No matter how fantastic the trappings may look, it would still be a *sign* hinting at a conscious thought, and not a symbol. A sign is always less than the thing it points to, and a symbol is always more than we can understand at first sight. Therefore we never stop at the sign but go on to the goal it indicates; but we remain with the symbol because it promises more than it reveals.

483　　If the contents of dreams agree with a sex theory, then we know their essence already, but if they are symbolic we at least know that we do not understand them yet. *A symbol does not disguise, it reveals in time.* It is obvious that dream interpretation will yield one result when you consider the dream to be symbolic, and an entirely different one when you assume that the essential thought is merely disguised but already known in principle. In the latter case, dream interpretation makes no sense whatever, for you find only what you know already. Therefore I always advise my pupils: "Learn as much as you can about symbolism and forget it all when you are analysing a dream." This advice is so important in practice that I myself have made it a rule to admit that I never understand a dream well enough to interpret it correctly. I do this in order to check the flow of my own associations and reactions, which might otherwise prevail over my patient's uncertainties and hesitations. As it is of the highest therapeutic importance for the analyst to get the message of the dream as accurately as possible, it is essential for him to explore the context of the dream-images with the utmost thoroughness. I had a dream while I was working with Freud that illustrates this very clearly.

484    I dreamt that I was in "my house," apparently on the first floor, in a cosy, pleasant drawing-room furnished in the style of the eighteenth century. I was rather astonished because I realized I had never seen this room before, and began to wonder what the ground floor was like. I went downstairs and found it rather dark, with panelled walls and heavy furniture dating from the sixteenth century or even earlier. I was greatly surprised and my curiosity increased, because it was all a very unexpected discovery. In order to become better acquainted with the whole structure of the house, I thought I would go down to the cellar. I found a door, with a flight of stone steps that led down to a large vaulted room. The floor consisted of large slabs of stone, and the walls struck me as very ancient. I examined the mortar and found it was mixed with splinters of brick. Obviously it was an old Roman wall. I began to grow excited. In a corner, I saw an iron ring in one of the stone slabs. I lifted it up and saw yet another narrow flight of steps leading down to a sort of cave which was obviously a prehistoric tomb. It contained two skulls, some bones, and broken shards of pottery. Then I woke up.

485    If Freud, when analysing this dream, had followed my method of exploring the context, he would have heard a far-reaching story. But I am afraid he would have dismissed it as a mere attempt to escape from a problem that was really his own. The dream is in fact a short summary of my life—the life of my mind. I grew up in a house two hundred years old, our furniture consisted mostly of pieces about a hundred years old, and mentally my greatest adventure had been the study of Kant and Schopenhauer. The great news of the day was the work of Charles Darwin. Shortly before this I had been living in a still medieval world with my parents, where the world and man were still presided over by divine omnipotence and providence. This world had become antiquated and obsolete. My Christian faith had been relativized by my encounter with Eastern religions and

Greek philosophy. It is for this reason that the ground floor was so still, dark, and obviously uninhabited.

486    My then historical interests had developed from my original preoccupation with comparative anatomy and paleontology when I worked as an assistant at the Anatomical Institute. I was fascinated by the bones of fossil man, particularly by the much-discussed *Neanderthalensis* and the still more controversial skull of Dubois' *Pithecanthropus*. As a matter of fact, these were my real associations to the dream. But I did not dare mention the subject of skulls, skeletons, or corpses to Freud, because I had learned that this theme was not popular with him. He cherished the peculiar idea that I anticipated his early death. He drew this conclusion from the fact that I was interested in the mummified corpses in the so-called Bleikeller in Bremen, which we had visited together in 1909 on our trip to America.[1]

487    Thus I was reluctant to come out with my thoughts, since through recent experience I was deeply impressed by the almost unbridgeable gap between Freud's mental outlook and background and my own. I was afraid of losing his friendship if I should open up to him about my inner world, which, I surmised, would look very queer to him. Feeling quite uncertain about my own psychology, I almost automatically told him a lie about my "free associations" in order to escape the impossible task of enlightening him about my very personal and utterly different mental constitution.

488    I soon realized that Freud was seeking for some incompatible wish of mine. And so I suggested tentatively that the skulls might refer to certain members of my family whose death, for some reason, I might desire. This proposal met with his approval, but I was not satisfied with such a "phoney" solution.

489    While I was trying to find a suitable answer to Freud's questions, I was suddenly confounded by an intuition about the role which the subjective factor plays in psychological understanding. My intuition was so overwhelming that my only thought was how to get out of this impossible snarl, and I took the easy way out by a lie. This was neither elegant nor morally defensible, but otherwise I should have risked a fatal row with Freud —and I did not feel up to that for many reasons.

1 For further details, see my *Memories, Dreams, Reflections*, pp. 156ff. (London edn., pp. 152ff.).

490   My intuition consisted in a sudden and most unexpected insight into the fact that my dream meant myself, *my* life and *my* world, my whole reality as against a theoretical structure erected by another, alien mind for reasons and purposes of its own. It was not Freud's dream, it was mine; and suddenly I understood in a flash what my dream meant.

491   I must apologize for this rather lengthy narration of the jam I got into through telling Freud my dream. But it is a good example of the difficulties in which one gets involved in the course of a real dream analysis. So much depends on the personal differences between the analyst and the analysand.

492   Dream analysis on this level is less a technique than a dialectical process between two personalities. If it is handled as a technique, the peculiarity of the subject as an individual is excluded and the therapeutic problem is reduced to the simple question: who will dominate whom? I had given up hypnotic treatment for this very reason, because I did not want to impose my will on others. I wanted the healing processes to grow out of the patient's own personality, and not out of suggestions of mine that would have only a passing effect. I wanted to protect and preserve my patient's dignity and freedom so that he could live his life by his own volition.

493   I could not share Freud's almost exclusive interest in sex. Assuredly sex plays no small role among human motives, but in many cases it is secondary to hunger, the power drive, ambition, fanaticism, envy, revenge, or the devouring passion of the creative impulse and the religious spirit.

494   For the first time it dawned on me that before we construct general theories about man and his psyche we should learn a great deal more about the real human being, rather than an abstract idea of *Homo sapiens*.

## 4. THE PROBLEM OF TYPES IN DREAM INTERPRETATION

495    In all other branches of science, it is a legitimate procedure to apply an hypothesis to an impersonal object. Psychology, however, inescapably confronts us with the living relationship between two individuals, neither of whom can be divested of his subjectivity or depersonalized in any way. They can mutually agree to deal with a chosen theme in an impersonal, objective manner, but when the whole of the personality becomes the object of their discussion, two individual subjects confront one another and the application of a one-way rule is excluded. Progress is possible only if mutual agreement can be reached. The objectivity of the final result can be established only by comparison with the standards that are generally valid in the social milieu to which the individuals belong, and we must also take their own mental equilibrium, or "sanity," into account. This does not mean that the final result must be the complete collectivization of the individual, for this would be a most unnatural condition. On the contrary, a sane and normal society is one in which people habitually disagree. General agreement is relatively rare outside the sphere of the instinctive qualities. Disagreement functions as a vehicle of mental life in a society, but it is not a goal; agreement is equally important. Because psychology basically depends upon balanced opposites, no judgment can be considered final unless allowance is made for its reversibility. The reason for this peculiarity lies in the fact that there is no standpoint above or outside psychology that would enable us to form a final judgment as to what the psyche is. Everything we can imagine is in a psychic state, i.e., in the state of a conscious representation. To get outside this is the whole difficulty of the physical sciences.

496     In spite of the fact that the only reality is the individual, some generalities are necessary in order to clarify and classify the empirical material, for it would obviously be impossible to formulate any psychological theory, or to teach it, by describing individuals. As a principle of classification, one can choose any likeness or unlikeness if only it is general enough, be it anatomical, physiological, or psychological. For our purpose, which is mainly concerned with psychology, it will be a psychological one, namely the widespread and easily observable fact that a great number of people are *extraverted* and others *introverted*. There is no need for a special explanation of these terms as they have passed into common speech.

497     This is one of the many generalities from which one can choose, and it is fairly suitable for our purpose in so far as we are seeking to describe the method of, and approach to, an understanding of dreams as the main source of natural symbols. As I have said, the process of interpretation consists in the confrontation of two minds, the analyst's and the analysand's, and not in the application of a preconceived theory. The analyst's mind is characterized by a number of individual peculiarities, perhaps just as many as the analysand's. They have the effect of prejudices. It cannot be assumed that the analyst is a superman just because he is a doctor and possesses a theory and a corresponding technique. He can only imagine himself to be superior if he assumes that his theory and technique are absolute truths, capable of embracing the whole of the psyche. Since such an assumption is more than doubtful, he cannot really be sure of it. Consequently he will be assailed by secret doubts in adopting such an attitude, i.e., in confronting the human wholeness of the analysand with a theory and a technique (which are mere hypotheses) instead of with his own living wholeness. This alone is the equivalent of his analysand's personality. Psychological experience and knowledge are nothing more than professional advantages on the part of the analyst that do not keep him safely outside the fray. He will be tested just as much as the analysand.

498     Since the systematic analysis of dreams demands the confrontation of two individuals, it will make a great difference whether their type of attitude is the same or not. If both belong to the same type, they may sail along happily for a long time. But if one is an extravert and the other an introvert, their different

and contradictory standpoints may clash right away, particularly when they are unconscious of their own type or are convinced that it is the only right one. Such a mistake is easily made, because the value of the one is the non-value of the other. The one will choose the majority view, the other will reject it just because it is everybody's taste. Freud himself interpreted the introverted type as an individual morbidly engrossed in himself. But introspection and self-knowledge can just as well be of the greatest value.

499 The apparently trifling difference between the extravert, with his emphasis on externals, and the introvert, who puts the emphasis on the way he takes a situation, plays a very great role in the analysis of dreams. From the start you must bear in mind that what the one appreciates may be very negative to the other, and the high ideal of the one can be an object of repulsion to the other. This becomes more and more obvious the further you go into the details of type differences. Extraversion and introversion are just two among many peculiarities of human behaviour, but they are often rather obvious and easily recognizable. If one studies extraverted individuals, for instance, one soon discovers that they differ from one another in many ways, and that being extraverted is a superficial and too general criterion to be really characteristic. That is why, long ago, I tried to find some further basic peculiarities that might serve the purpose of getting some order into the apparently limitless variations of human personality.

500 I had always been impressed by the fact that there are surprisingly many individuals who never use their minds if they can avoid it, and yet are not stupid, and an equal number who obviously do use their minds but in an amazingly stupid way. I was also surprised to find many intelligent and wide-awake people who lived (as far as one could make out) as if they had never learned to use their sense organs. They did not see the things before their eyes, hear the words sounding in their ears, notice the things they touched or tasted, and lived without being aware of their own bodies. There were others who seemed to live in a most curious condition of consciousness, as if the state they had arrived at today were final, with no change in sight, or as if the world and the psyche were static and would remain so for ever. They seemed devoid of all imagination, and entirely and exclu-

sively dependent on sense perception. Chances and possibilities did not exist in their world, and in their "today" there was no real "tomorrow." The future was just the repetition of the past.

501     What I am trying to convey to the reader is the first glimpse of the impressions I received when I began to observe the many people I met. It soon became clear to me that the people who used their minds were those who *thought,* who employed their intellectual faculty in trying to adapt to people and circumstances; and that the equally intelligent people, who yet did not think, were those who sought and found their way by *feeling.* Now "feeling" is a word that needs some explanation. For instance, one speaks of "feeling" when it is a matter of "sentiment" (corresponding to the French *sentiment*). But one also applies the same word to an opinion; a communication from the White House may begin: "The President feels . . ." Or one uses it to express an intuition: "I had a feeling . . ." Finally, feeling is often confused with sensation.

502     What I mean by feeling in contrast to thinking is a *judgment of value:* agreeable or disagreeable, good or bad, and so on. Feeling so defined is not an emotion or affect, which is, as the words convey, an involuntary manifestation. Feeling as I mean it is a judgment without any of the obvious bodily reactions that characterize an emotion. Like thinking, it is a *rational* function; whereas intuition, like sensation, is *irrational.* In so far as intuition is a "hunch" it is not a product of a voluntary act; it is rather an involuntary event, which depends on different external or internal circumstances instead of an act of judgment. Intuition is more like sense perception, which is also an irrational event in so far as it depends essentially on external or internal stimuli deriving from physical and not mental causes.

503     These four functional types correspond to the obvious means by which consciousness obtains its orientation. *Sensation* (or sense perception) tells you that something exists; *thinking* tells you what it is; *feeling* tells you whether it is agreeable or not; and *intuition* tells you where it comes from and where it is going.

504     The reader should understand that these four criteria are just so many viewpoints among others, such as will-power, temperament, imagination, memory, morality, religiousness, etc.

There is nothing dogmatic about them, nor do they claim to be the ultimate truth about psychology; but their basic nature recommends them as suitable principles of classification. Classification has little value if it does not provide a means of orientation and a practical terminology. I find classification into types particularly helpful when I am called upon to explain parents to children or husbands to wives, and vice versa. It is also useful in understanding one's own prejudices.

505     Thus, if you want to understand another person's dream, you have to sacrifice your own predilections and suppress your prejudices, at least for the time being. This is neither easy nor comfortable, because it means a moral effort that is not everyone's cup of tea. But, if you do not make the effort to criticize your own standpoint and to admit its relativity, you will get neither the right information about, nor sufficient insight into, your analysand's mind. As you expect at least some willingness on his part to listen to your opinion and to take it seriously, the patient must be granted the same right too. Although such a relationship is indispensable for any understanding and is therefore a self-evident necessity, one has to remind oneself again and again that in therapy it is more important for the patient to understand than for the analyst's theoretical expectations to be satisfied. The patient's resistance to the analyst is not necessarily wrong; it is rather a sign that something does not "click." Either the patient is not yet at a point where he would be able to understand, or the interpretation does not fit.

506     In our efforts to interpret the dream symbols of another person, we are particularly hampered by an almost invincible tendency to fill the gaps in our understanding by *projection*—that is, by the assumption that what I think is also my partner's thought. This source of error can be avoided by establishing the context of the dream-images and excluding all theoretical assumptions—except for the heuristic hypothesis that dreams somehow make sense.

507     There is no rule, let alone a law, of dream interpretation, although it does look as if the general purpose of dreams is *compensation*. At least, compensation can be said to be the most promising and most fertile hypothesis. Sometimes the manifest dream demonstrates its compensatory character from the start. For instance, a patient with no small idea of himself and his

moral superiority dreamt of a drunken tramp wallowing in a ditch beside the road. The dreamer says (in the dream): "It's awful to see how low a man can fall!" It is evident that the dream was attempting to deflate his exalted opinion of himself. But there was more to it than that. It turned out that he had a black sheep in the family, a younger brother who was a degenerate alcoholic. What the dream also revealed was that his superior attitude compensated the inferiority of his brother—and of the brother who was also himself.

508    In another case, a lady who was proud of her intelligent understanding of psychology kept on dreaming about a certain woman whom she occasionally met in society. In real life she did not like her, thinking her vain, dishonest, and an intriguer. She wondered why she should dream of a person so unlike herself and yet, in the dream, so friendly and intimate, like a sister. The dream obviously wanted to convey the idea that she was "shadowed" by an unconscious character resembling that woman. As she had a very definite idea of herself, she was unaware of her own power-complex and her own shady motives, which had more than once led to disagreeable scenes that were always attributed to others but never to her own machinations.

509    It is not only the shadow-side that is overlooked, disregarded and repressed; positive qualities can also be subjected to the same treatment. An instance of this would be an apparently modest, self-effacing man with winning, apologetic or deprecatory manners, who always takes a back seat though with seeming politeness he never misses an opportunity to be present. His judgment is well-informed, even competent and apparently appreciative, yet it hints at a certain higher level from which the matter in question could be dealt with in a far superior way. In his dreams he constantly meets great men such as Napoleon and Alexander the Great. His obvious inferiority complex is clearly compensated by such momentous visitors, but at the same time the dreams raise the critical question: what sort of man must I be to have such illustrious callers? In this respect, they show that the dreamer nurses a secret megalomania as an antidote to his inferiority complex. Without his knowing it, the idea of grandeur enables him to immunize himself against all influences from his surroundings; nothing penetrates his skin, and he can thus keep aloof from obligations that would be binding to other

people. He does not feel in any way called upon to prove to himself or his fellows that his superior judgment is based on corresponding merits. He is not only a bachelor, but mentally sterile as well. He only understands the art of spreading hints and whisperings about his importance, but no monument witnesses to his deeds. He plays this inane game all unconsciously, and the dreams try to bring it home to him in a curiously ambiguous way, as the old saying goes: *Ducunt volentem fata, nolentem trahunt* (the fates lead the willing, but drag the unwilling). Hobnobbing with Napoleon or being on speaking terms with Alexander the Great is just the thing a man with an inferiority complex could wish for—a wholesale confirmation of the greatness behind the scenes. It is true wish-fulfilment, which anticipates an achievement without the merits that should lead to it. But why, one will ask, can't dreams be open and direct about it, and say it clearly without subterfuges that seem to mislead in an almost cunning way?

510    I have frequently been asked this question and I have asked it myself. I am often surprised at the tantalizing way dreams seem to evade definite information or omit the decisive point. Freud assumed the existence of a special factor, called the "censor," which was supposed to twist the dream-images and make them unrecognizable or misleading in order to deceive the dreaming consciousness about the real subject of the dream: the incompatible wish. Through the concealment of the critical point, it was supposed that the dreamer's sleep would be protected against the shock of a disagreeable reminiscence. But the dream as a guardian of sleep is an unlikely hypothesis, since dreams just as often disturb sleep.

511    It looks rather as if, instead of an unconscious censor, consciousness, or the dreamer's approach to consciousness, had itself a blotting-out effect on the subliminal contents. Subliminality corresponds to what Janet calls *abaissement du niveau mental*. It is a lowering of the energic tension, in which psychic contents sink below the threshold and lose the qualities they possess in their conscious state. They lose their definiteness and clearness, and their relations become vaguely analogous instead of rational and comprehensible. This is a phenomenon that can be observed in all dreamlike conditions, whether due to fatigue, fever, or toxins. But as soon as their tension increases, they become less

subliminal, more definite, and thus more conscious. There is no reason to believe that the *abaissement* shields incompatible wishes from discovery, although it may incidentally happen that an incompatible wish disappears along with the vanishing consciousness. The dream, being essentially a subliminal process, cannot produce a definite thought, unless it should cease to be a dream by instantly becoming a conscious content. The dream cannot but skip all those points that are particularly important to the conscious mind. It manifests the "fringe of consciousness," like the faint glimmer of the stars during a total eclipse of the sun.

512    Dream symbols are for the most part manifestations of a psyche that is beyond the control of consciousness. Meaning and purposefulness are not prerogatives of the conscious mind; they operate through the whole of living nature. There is no difference in principle between organic and psychic formations. As a plant produces its flower, so the psyche creates its symbols. Every dream is evidence of this process. Thus, through dreams, intuitions, impulses, and other spontaneous happenings, instinctive forces influence the activity of consciousness. Whether that influence is for better or worse depends on the actual contents of the unconscious. If it contains too many things that normally ought to be conscious, then its function becomes twisted and prejudiced; motives appear that are not based on true instincts, but owe their activity to the fact that they have been consigned to the unconscious by repression or neglect. They overlay, as it were, the normal unconscious psyche and distort its natural symbol-producing function.

513    Therefore it is usual for psychotherapy, concerned as it is with the causes of a disturbance, to begin by eliciting from the patient a more or less voluntary confession of all the things he dislikes, is ashamed of, or fears. This is like the much older confession in the Church, which in many ways anticipated modern psychological techniques. In practice, however, the procedure is often reversed, since overpowering feelings of inferiority or a serious weakness may make it very difficult, if not impossible, for the patient to face a still deeper darkness and worthlessness. I have often found it more profitable first to give a positive outlook to the patient, a foundation on which he could stand, before we approached more painful and debilitating insights.

514     Take as a simple example the dream of "personal exalta-
tion," in which one has tea with the Queen of England, or is on
intimate terms with the Pope. If the dreamer is not a schizo-
phrenic, the practical interpretation of the symbol depends very
much on the state of his consciousness. If he is obviously convinced of his greatness a damper will be indicated, but if it is a
matter of a worm already crushed by the weight of his inferiority, a further lowering of his values would amount to cruelty. In
the former case a reductive treatment will recommend itself,
and it will be easy to show from the associative material how
inappropriate and childish the dreamer's intentions are, and
how much they emanate from infantile wishes to be equal or
superior to his parents. But in the latter case, where an all-
pervading feeling of worthlessness has already devalued every
positive aspect, to show the dreamer, on top of it all, how infantile, ridiculous, or even perverse he is would be quite unfitting.
Such a procedure would only increase his inferiority, as well as
cause an unwelcome and quite unnecessary resistance to the
treatment.

515     There is no therapeutic technique or doctrine that is generally applicable, since every case that comes for treatment is an
individual in a specific condition. I remember a patient I had to
treat over a period of nine years. I saw him only for a few weeks
each year, as he lived abroad. From the start I knew what his real
trouble was, but I also saw how the least attempt to get closer to
the truth was met by a violent reaction and a self-defence that
threatened complete rupture between us. Whether I liked it or
not, I had to do my best to maintain the rapport and to follow
his inclination, supported by his dreams, though this led the discussion away from the central problem that, according to all reasonable expectations, should have been discussed. It went so far
that I often accused myself of leading my patient astray, and
only the fact that his condition slowly but clearly improved pre-
vented me from confronting him brutally with the truth.

516     In the tenth year, however, the patient declared himself
cured and freed from all symptoms. I was surprised and ready to
doubt his statement, because theoretically he could not be
cured. Noticing my astonishment, he smiled and said: "And now
I want to thank you quite particularly for your unfailing tact
and patience in helping me to circumvent the painful cause of

my neurosis. I am now ready to tell you everything about it. If I had been able to do so I would have told you right out at the first consultation. But that would have destroyed my rapport with you, and where would I have been then? I would have been morally bankrupt and would have lost the ground from under my feet, having nothing to stand on. In the course of the years I have learnt to trust you, and as my confidence grew my condition improved. I improved because my belief in myself was restored, and now I am strong enough to discuss the problem that was destroying me."

517    He then made a devastatingly frank confession, which showed me the reasons for the peculiar course our treatment had followed. The original shock had been such that he could not face it alone. It needed the two of us, and that was the therapeutic task, not the fulfilment of theoretical presuppositions.

518    From cases like this I learnt to follow the lines already indicated in the material presented by the patient and in his disposition, rather than commit myself to general theoretical considerations that might not be applicable to that particular case. The practical knowledge of human nature I have accumulated in the course of sixty years has taught me to regard each case as a new experience, for which, first of all, I have to seek the individual approach. Sometimes I have not hesitated to plunge into a careful study of infantile events and fantasies; at other times I have begun at the top, even if this meant soaring into a mist of most unlikely metaphysical speculations. It all depends on whether I am able to learn the language of the patient and to follow the gropings of his unconscious towards the light. Some demand one thing and some another. Such are the differences between individuals.

519    This is eminently true of the interpretation of symbols. Two different individuals can have almost the same dream, yet if one is young and the other old, the problems disturbing them will be correspondingly different, and it would be absurd to interpret both dreams in the same way. An example that comes to mind is a dream in which a company of young men are riding on horseback across a wide field. The dreamer is in the lead and jumps a ditch of water, just clearing it. The others fall into the ditch. The young man who told me this dream was a cautious, introverted type and rather afraid of adventure. But the old

man, who also had this dream, was bold and fearless, and had lived an active and enterprising life. At the time of the dream, he was an invalid who would not settle down, gave much trouble to his doctor and nurse, and had injured himself by his disobedience and restlessness. Obviously the dream was telling the young man what he *ought* to do, and the old man what he was *still doing*. While it encouraged the hesitant young man, the old one would be only too glad to risk the jump. But that still-flickering spirit of adventure was just his greatest trouble.

520     This example shows how the interpretation of dreams and symbols depends largely on the individual disposition of the dreamer. Symbols have not one meaning only but several, and often they even characterize a pair of opposites, as does, for instance, the *stella matutina*, the morning star, which is a well-known symbol of Christ and at the same time of the devil (Lucifer). The same applies to the lion. The correct interpretation depends on the context, i.e., the associations connected with the image, and on the actual condition of the dreamer's mind.

## 5. THE ARCHETYPE IN DREAM SYMBOLISM

521    The hypothesis we have advanced, that dreams serve the purpose of *compensation,* is a very broad and comprehensive assumption. It means that we believe the dream to be a normal psychic phenomenon that transmits unconscious reactions or spontaneous impulses to the conscious mind. Since only a small minority of dreams are manifestly compensatory, we must pay particular attention to the language of dreams that we consider to be symbolic. The study of this language is almost a science in itself. It has. as we have seen, an infinite variety of individual expressions. They can be read with the help of the dreamer, who himself provides the associative material, or context of the dream-image, so that we can look at all its aspects as if circumambulating it. This method proves to be sufficient in all ordinary cases, such as when a relative, a friend, or a patient tells you a dream more or less conversationally. But when it is a matter of outstanding dreams, of obsessive or recurrent dreams, or dreams that are highly emotional, the personal associations produced by the dreamer no longer suffice for a satisfactory interpretation. In such cases, we have to take into consideration the fact, already observed and commented on by Freud, that elements often occur in a dream that are not individual and cannot be derived from personal experience. They are what Freud called "archaic remnants"—thought-forms whose presence cannot be explained by anything in the individual's own life, but seem to be aboriginal, innate, and inherited patterns of the human mind.

522    Just as the human body represents a whole museum of organs, with a long evolutionary history behind them, so we should expect the mind to be organized in a similar way rather than to be a product without history. By "history" I do not mean the fact that the mind builds itself up through conscious tradition (language, etc.), but rather its biological, prehistoric,

and unconscious development beginning with archaic man, whose psyche was still similar to that of an animal. This immensely old psyche forms the basis of our mind, just as the structure of our body is erected upon a generally mammalian anatomy. Wherever the trained eye of the morphologist looks, it recognizes traces of the original pattern. Similarly, the experienced investigator of the psyche cannot help seeing the analogies between dream-images and the products of the primitive mind, its *représentations collectives,* or mythological motifs. But just as the morphologist needs the science of comparative anatomy, so the psychologist cannot do without a "comparative anatomy of the psyche." He must have a sufficient experience of dreams and other products of the unconscious on the one hand, and on the other of mythology in its widest sense. He cannot even see the analogy between a case of compulsion neurosis, schizophrenia, or hysteria and that of a classical demonic possession if he has not sufficient knowledge of both.

523    My views about the "archaic remnants," which I have called "archetypes" [1] or "primordial images," are constantly criticized by people who lack a sufficient knowledge both of the psychology of dreams and of mythology. The term "archetype" is often misunderstood as meaning a certain definite mythological image or motif. But this would be no more than a conscious representation, and it would be absurd to assume that such variable representations could be inherited. The archetype is, on the contrary, an inherited *tendency* of the human mind to form representations of mythological motifs—representations that vary a great deal without losing their basic pattern. There are, for instance, numerous representations of the motif of the hostile brothers, but the motif remains the same. This inherited tendency is instinctive, like the specific impulse of nest-building, migration, etc. in birds. One finds these *représentations collectives* practically everywhere, characterized by the same or similar motifs. They cannot be assigned to any particular time or region or race. They are without known origin, and they can reproduce themselves even where transmission through migration must be ruled out.

524    My critics have also incorrectly assumed that by archetypes I

1 From Gk. *archē,* 'origin', and *tupos,* 'blow, imprint'.

mean "inherited ideas," and on this ground have dismissed the concept of the archetype as a mere superstition. But if archetypes were ideas that originated in our conscious mind or were acquired by it, one would certainly understand them, and would not be astonished and bewildered when they appear in consciousness. I can remember many cases of people who have consulted me because they were baffled by their own or their children's dreams. The reason was that the dreams contained images that could not be traced to anything they remembered, and they could not explain where their children could have picked up such strange and incomprehensible ideas. These people were highly educated persons, sometimes psychiatrists themselves. One of them was a professor who had a sudden vision and thought he was crazy. He came to me in a state of complete panic. I simply took a four-hundred-year-old volume from the shelf and showed him an old woodcut that depicted his vision. "You don't need to be crazy," I told him. "They knew all about your vision four hundred years ago." Whereupon he sat down entirely deflated but once more normal.

525    I particularly remember the case of a man who was himself a psychiatrist. He brought me a handwritten booklet he had received as a Christmas present from his ten-year-old daughter. It contained a whole series of dreams she had had when she was eight years old. It was the weirdest series I had ever seen, and I could well understand why her father was more than puzzled by the dreams. Childlike though they were, they were a bit uncanny, containing images whose origin was wholly incomprehensible to her father. Here are the salient motifs from the dreams:[2]

1. The "bad animal": a snakelike monster with many horns, that kills and devours all other animals. But God comes from the four corners, being really four gods, and gives rebirth to all the animals.

2. Ascent into heaven where pagan dances are being celebrated, and descent to hell where angels are doing good deeds.

3. A horde of small animals frightens the dreamer. The animals grow to enormous size, and one of them devours her.

4. A small mouse is penetrated by worms, snakes, fishes, and hu-

---

[2] [For another analysis of this case, see Jacobi, Complex/Archetype/Symbol (1959), Part II.—EDITORS.]

man beings. Thus the mouse becomes human. This is the origin of mankind in four stages.

5. A drop of water is looked at through a microscope: it is full of branches. This is the origin of the world.

6. A bad boy with a clod of earth. He throws bits of it at the passers-by, and they all become bad too.

7. A drunken woman falls into the water and comes out sober and renewed.

8. In America many people are rolling in an ant heap, attacked by the ants. The dreamer, in a panic, falls into a river.

9. The dreamer is in a desert on the moon. She sinks so deep into the ground that she reaches hell.

10. She touches a luminous ball seen in a vision. Vapours come out of it. Then a man comes and kills her.

11. She is dangerously ill. Suddenly birds come out of her skin and cover her completely.

12. Swarms of gnats hide the sun, moon, and stars, all except one star which then falls on the dreamer.

526    In the unabridged German original, each dream begins with the words of the fairytale: "Once upon a time . . ." With these words the little dreamer suggests that she feels as if each dream were a sort of fairytale, which she wants to tell her father as a Christmas present. Her father was unable to elucidate the dreams through their context, for there seemed to be no personal associations. Indeed, this kind of childhood dream often seems to be a "Just So Story," with very few or no spontaneous associations. The possibility that these dreams were conscious elaborations can of course be ruled out only by someone who had an intimate knowledge of the child's character and did not doubt her truthfulness. They would, however, remain a challenge to our understanding even if they were fantasies that originated in the waking state. The father was convinced that they were authentic, and I have no reason to doubt it. I knew the little girl myself, but this was before she gave the dreams to her father, and I had no chance to question her about them, for she lived far away from Switzerland and died of an infectious disease about a year after that Christmas.

527    The dreams have a decidedly peculiar character, for their leading thoughts are in a way like philosophical problems. The first dream, for instance, speaks of an evil monster killing all other animals, but God gives rebirth to them through a kind of

*apocatastasis,* or restitution. In the Western world this idea is known through Christian tradition. It can be found in the Acts of the Apostles 3:21: "(Christ,) whom the heaven must receive until the times of restitution of all things . . ." The early Greek Fathers of the Church (Origen, for instance) particularly insisted on the idea that, at the end of time, everything will be restored by the Redeemer to its original and perfect state. According to Matthew 17:11, there was already an old Jewish tradition that Elias "truly shall first come, and restore all things." I Corinthians 15:22 refers to the same idea in the following words: "For as in Adam all die, even so in Christ shall all be made alive."

528    One might argue that the child had met with this thought in her religious education. But she had had very little of this, as her parents (Protestants) belonged to those people, common enough in our days, who know the Bible only from hearsay. It is particularly unlikely that the idea of *apocatastasis* had been explained to her, and had become a matter of vital interest. Her father, at any rate, was entirely unaware of this mythical idea.

529    Nine of the twelve dreams are concerned with the theme of destruction and restoration. We find the same connection in I Corinthians 15:22, where Adam and Christ, i.e., death and resurrection, are linked together. None of these dreams, however, shows anything more than superficial traces of a specifically Christian education or influence. On the contrary, they show more analogy with primitive tales. This is corroborated by the other motif—the cosmogonic myth of the creation of the world and of man, which appears in dreams 4 and 5.

530    The idea of Christ the Redeemer belongs to the world-wide and pre-Christian motif of the hero and rescuer who, although devoured by the monster, appears again in a miraculous way, having overcome the dragon or whale or whatever it was that swallowed him. How, when, and where such a motif originated nobody knows. We do not even know how to set about investigating the problem in a sound way. Our only certainty is that every generation, so far as we can see, has found it as an old tradition. Thus we can safely assume that the motif "originated" at a time when man did not yet know that he possessed a hero myth—in an age, therefore, when he did not yet reflect con-

sciously on what he was saying. The hero figure is a typical image, an archetype, which has existed since time immemorial.

531      The best examples of the spontaneous production of archetypal images are presented by individuals, particularly children, who live in a milieu where one can be sufficiently certain that any direct knowledge of the tradition is out of the question. The milieu in which our little dreamer lived was acquainted only with the Christian tradition, and very superficially at that. Christian traces may be represented in her dreams by such ideas as God, angels, heaven, hell, and evil, but the way in which they are treated points to a tradition that is entirely non-Christian.

532      Let us take the first dream, of the God who really consists of four gods, coming from the "four corners." The corners of what? There is no room mentioned in the dream. A room would not even fit in with the picture of what is obviously a cosmic event, in which the Universal Being himself intervenes. The quaternity itself is a strange idea, but one that plays a great role in Eastern religions and philosophies. In the Christian tradition it has been superseded by the Trinity, a notion that we must assume was known to the child. But who in an ordinary middle-class milieu would be likely to know of a divine quaternity? It is an idea that was once current in circles acquainted with Hermetic philosophy in the Middle Ages, but it petered out at the beginning of the eighteenth century and has been entirely obsolete for at least two hundred years. Where, then, did the little girl pick it up? From Ezekiel's vision? But there is no Christian teaching that identifies the seraphim with God.

533      The same question may be asked about the horned serpent. In the Bible, it is true, there are many horned animals, for instance in the Book of Revelation (ch. 13). But they seem to be quadrupeds, although their overlord is the dragon, which in Greek (*drakon*) means serpent. The horned serpent appears in Latin alchemy as the *quadricornutus serpens* (four-horned serpent), a symbol of Mercurius and an antagonist of the Christian Trinity. But this is an obscure reference, and, as far as I can discover, it occurs only in one author.[3]

534      In dream 2 a motif appears that is definitely non-Christian and a reversal of values: pagan dances by men in heaven and

---

3 [Gerard Dorn, of Frankfurt, a 17th-century physician and alchemist.]

good deeds by angels in hell. This suggests, if anything, a relativization of moral values. Where did the child hit on such a revolutionary and modern idea, worthy of Nietzsche's genius? Such an idea is not strange to the philosophical mind of the East, but where could we find it in the child's milieu, and what is its place in the mind of an eight-year-old girl?

535    This question leads to a further one: what is the compensatory meaning of the dreams, to which the little girl obviously attributed so much importance that she gave them to her father as a Christmas present?

536    If the dreamer had been a primitive medicine-man, one would not go far wrong in supposing them to be variations on the philosophical themes of death, resurrection, or restitution, the origin of the world, the creation of man, and the relativity of values (Lao-tze: "high stands on low"). One might well give up such dreams as hopeless if one tried to interpret them from a personal standpoint. But, as I have said, they undoubtedly contain *représentations collectives,* and they are in a way analogous to the doctrines taught to young people in primitive tribes when they are initiated into manhood. At such times they learn about what God or the gods or the "founding" animals have done, how the world and man were created, what the end of the world will be, and the meaning of death. And when do we, in our Christian civilization, hand out similar instructions? At the beginning of adolescence. But many people begin to think of these things again in old age, at the approach of death.

537    Our dreamer, as it happened, was in both these situations, for she was approaching puberty and at the same time the end of her life. Little or nothing in the symbolism of the dreams points to the beginning of a normal adult life, but there are many allusions to destruction and restoration. When I first read the dreams, I had the uncanny feeling that they foreboded disaster. The reason I felt like that was the peculiar nature of the compensation that I deduced from the symbolism. It was the opposite of what one would expect to find in the consciousness of a girl of that age. These dreams open up a new and rather terrifying vision of life and death, such as one might expect in someone who looks back upon life rather than forward to its natural continuation. Their atmosphere recalls the old Roman saying, *vita somnium breve* (life is a short dream), rather than the joy and

exuberance of life's springtime. For this child, life was a *ver sacrum vovendum,* a vow of a vernal sacrifice. Experience shows that the unknown approach of death casts an *adumbratio,* an anticipatory shadow, over the life and dreams of the victim. Even the altar in our Christian churches represents, on the one hand, a tomb, and on the other a place of resurrection—the transformation of death into eternal life.

538    Such are the thoughts that the dreams brought home to the child. They were a preparation for death, expressed through short stories, like the instruction at primitive initiations, or the *koans* of Zen Buddhism. It is an instruction that does not resemble the orthodox Christian doctrine but is more like primitive thought. It seems to have originated outside the historical tradition, in the matrix that, since prehistoric times, has nourished philosophical and religious speculations about life and death.

539    In the case of this girl, it was as if future events were casting their shadow ahead by arousing thought-forms that, though normally dormant, are destined to describe or accompany the approach of a fatal issue. They are to be found everywhere and at all times. Although the concrete shape in which they express themselves is more or less personal, their general pattern is collective, just as animal instincts vary a good deal in different species and yet serve the same general purpose. We do not assume that each newborn animal creates its own instincts as an individual acquisition, and we cannot suppose, either, that human beings invent and produce their specifically human modes of reaction with every new birth. Like the instincts, the collective thought-patterns of the human mind are innate and inherited; and they function, when occasion arises, in more or less the same way in all of us.

540    Emotional manifestations are based on similar patterns, and are recognizably the same all over the earth. We understand them even in animals, and the animals themselves understand each other in this respect, even if they belong to different species. And what about insects, with their complicated symbiotic functions? Most of them do not even know their parents and have nobody to teach them. Why should we suppose, then, that man is the only living creature deprived of specific instincts, or that his psyche is devoid of all traces of its evolution? Naturally, if you identify the psyche with consciousness, you can easily suc-

cumb to the erroneous idea that the psyche is a *tabula rasa,* completely empty at birth, and that it later contains only what it has learnt by individual experience. But the psyche is more than consciousness. Animals have little consciousness, but they have many impulses and reactions that denote the existence of a psyche, and primitives do a lot of things whose meaning is unknown to them. You may ask many civilized people in vain for the reason and meaning of the Christmas tree or of the coloured eggs at Easter, because they have no idea about the meaning of these customs. The fact is, they do things without knowing why they do them. I am inclined to believe that things were generally done first and that only a long time afterwards somebody asked a question about them, and then eventually discovered why they were done. The medical psychologist is constantly confronted with otherwise intelligent patients who behave in a peculiar way and have no inkling of what they say or do. We have dreams whose meaning escapes us entirely, even though we may be firmly convinced that the dream has a definite meaning. We feel it is important or even terrifying, but why?

541    Regular observation of such facts has enforced the hypothesis of an unconscious psyche, the contents of which seem to be of approximately the same variety as those of consciousness. We know that consciousness depends in large measure on the collaboration of the unconscious. When you make a speech, the next sentence is being prepared while you speak, but this preparation is mostly unconscious. If the unconscious does not collaborate and withholds the next sentence you are stuck. You want to quote a name, or a term otherwise familiar to you, but nothing is forthcoming. The unconscious does not deliver it. You want to introduce somebody whom you know well, but his name has vanished, as if you had never known it. Thus you depend on the goodwill of your unconscious. Any time the unconscious chooses, it can defeat your otherwise good memory, or put something into your mouth that you did not intend at all. It can produce unpredictable and unreasonable moods and affects and thus cause all sorts of complications.

542    Superficially, such reactions and impulses seem to be of an intimately personal nature and are therefore believed to be entirely individual. In reality, they are based on a preformed and ever-ready instinctive system with its own characteristic and uni-

versally understandable thought-forms, reflexes, attitudes, and gestures. These follow a pattern that was laid down long before there was any trace of a reflective consciousness. It is even conceivable that the latter originated in violent emotional clashes and their often disastrous consequences. Take the case of the savage who, in a moment of anger and disappointment at having caught no fish, strangles his much beloved only son, and is then seized with immeasurable regret as he holds the little dead body in his arms. Such a man has a great chance to remember the agony of this moment for ever. This could have been the beginning of a reflective consciousness. At all events, the shock of a similar emotional experience is often needed to make people wake up and pay attention to what they are doing. I would mention the famous case of the Spanish hidalgo, Ramón Lull, who after a long chase finally succeeded in meeting his lady at a secret rendezvous. Silently she opened her garment and showed him her cancer-eaten bosom. The shock changed his life: he became a holy man.

543    Often in the case of these sudden transformations one can prove that an archetype has been at work for a long time in the unconscious, skilfully arranging circumstances that will unavoidably lead to a crisis. It is not rare for the development to manifest itself so clearly (for instance in a series of dreams) that the catastrophe can be predicted with reasonable certainty. One can conclude from experiences such as these that archetypal forms are not just static patterns, but dynamic factors that manifest themselves in spontaneous impulses, just as instincts do. Certain dreams, visions, or thoughts can suddenly appear, and in spite of careful investigation one cannot find out what causes them. This does not mean that they have no cause; they certainly have, but it is so remote or obscure that one cannot see what it is. One must wait until the dream and its meaning are sufficiently understood, or until some external event occurs that will explain the dream.

544    Our conscious thoughts often concern themselves with the future and its possibilities, and so does the unconscious and its dreams. There has long been a world-wide belief that the chief function of dreams is prognostication of the future. In antiquity, and still in the Middle Ages, dreams played their part in medical prognosis. I can confirm from a modern dream the

prognosis, or rather precognition, in an old dream quoted by Artemidoros of Daldis, in the second century A.D. He relates that a man dreamt he saw his father die in the flames of a house on fire. Not long afterwards, he himself died of a *phlegmone* (fire, high fever), presumably pneumonia. Now it so happened that a colleague of mine was suffering from a deadly gangrenous fever —in fact, a *phlegmone*. A former patient of his, who had no knowledge of the nature of the doctor's illness, dreamt that the doctor was perishing in a great fire. The dream occurred three weeks before the doctor died, at a time when he had just entered hospital and the disease was only at its beginning. The dreamer knew nothing but the bare fact that the doctor was ill and had entered hospital.

545　　As this example shows, dreams can have an anticipatory or prognostic aspect, and their interpreter will be well advised to take this aspect into account, particularly when an obviously meaningful dream does not yield a context sufficient to explain it. Such a dream often comes right out of the blue, and one wonders what could have prompted it. Of course, if one knew its ultimate outcome, the cause would be clear. It is only our conscious mind that does not know; the unconscious seems already informed, and to have submitted the case to a careful prognostic examination, more or less in the way consciousness would have done if it had known the relevant facts. But, precisely because they were subliminal, they could be perceived by the unconscious and submitted to a sort of examination that anticipates their ultimate result. So far as one can make out from dreams, the unconscious in its "deliberations" proceeds in an instinctive way rather than along rational lines. The latter way is the prerogative of consciousness, which selects with reason and knowledge. But the unconscious is guided chiefly by instinctive trends, represented by corresponding thought-forms—the archetypes. It looks as if it were a poet who had been at work rather than a rational doctor, who would speak of infection, fever, toxins, etc., whereas the dream describes the diseased body as a man's earthly house, and the fever as the heat of a conflagration that is destroying the house and its inhabitant.

546　　As this dream shows, the archetypal mind has handled the situation in the same way as it did at the time of Artemidoros. A situation of a more or less unknown nature has been intuitively grasped by the unconscious and submitted to an archetypal treatment. This shows clearly that, in place of the *raisonnement* which consciousness would have applied, the archetypal mind has autonomously taken over the task of prognostication. The archetypes have their own initiative and their own specific energy, which enable them not only to produce a meaningful interpretation (in their own style) but also to intervene in a given situation with their own impulses and thought-forms. In this respect they function like complexes, which also enjoy a certain autonomy in everyday life. They come and go very much as they please, and they often interfere with our conscious intentions in an embarrassing way.

547     One can perceive the specific energy of the archetypes when one experiences the peculiar feeling of numinosity that accompanies them—the fascination or spell that emanates from them. This is also characteristic of the personal complexes, whose behaviour may be compared with the role played by the archetypal *représentations collectives* in the social life of all times. As personal complexes have their individual history, so do social complexes of an archetypal character. But while personal complexes never produce more than a personal bias, archetypes create myths, religions, and philosophical ideas that influence and set their stamp on whole nations and epochs. And just as the products of personal complexes can be understood as compensations of onesided or faulty attitudes of consciousness, so myths of a religious nature can be interpreted as a sort of mental therapy for the sufferings of mankind, such as hunger, war, disease, old age, and death.

548     The universal hero myth, for example, shows the picture of a powerful man or god-man who vanquishes evil in the form of dragons, serpents, monsters, demons, and enemies of all kinds, and who liberates his people from destruction and death. The narration or ritual repetition of sacred texts and ceremonies, and the worship of such a figure with dances, music, hymns, prayers, and sacrifices, grip the audience with numinous emotions and exalt the participants to identification with the hero. If we contemplate such a situation with the eyes of a believer, we can understand how the ordinary man is gripped, freed from his impotence and misery, and raised to an almost superhuman status, at least for the time being, and often enough he is sus-

tained by such a conviction for a long time. An initiation of this kind produces a lasting impression, and may even create an attitude that gives a certain form and style to the life of a society. I would mention as an example the Eleusinian mysteries, which were finally suppressed at the beginning of the seventh century. They formed, together with the Delphic oracle, the essence and spirit of ancient Greece. On a much greater scale the Christian era owes its name and significance to another antique mystery, that of the god-man, which has its roots in the archetypal Osiris-Horus myth of ancient Egypt.

549    It is nowadays a common prejudice to assume that once, in an obscure prehistoric time, the basic mythological ideas were "invented" by a clever old philosopher or prophet, and ever afterwards "believed" by credulous and uncritical people, although the stories told by a power-seeking priesthood were not really "true" but mere "wishful thinking." The word "invent" is derived from the Latin *invenire* and means, in the first place, to "come upon" or to "find" something and, in the second, to find something by *seeking* for it. In the latter case, it is not a matter of finding or coming upon something by mere chance, for there is a sort of foreknowledge or a faint inkling of the thing you are going to find.

550    When we contemplate the strange ideas in the dreams of the little girl, it seems unlikely that she *sought* them, as she was rather surprised at finding them. They occurred to her rather as strange and unexpected stories that seemed noteworthy and interesting enough to be given to her father as a Christmas present. In doing so, she lifted them up into the sphere of our still living Christian mystery, the birth of our Lord, blended with the secret of the evergreen tree that carries the newborn Light. Although there is ample historical evidence for the symbolic relationship between Christ and the tree symbol, the little girl's parents would have been badly embarrassed had they been asked to explain exactly what they meant by decorating a tree with burning candles to celebrate the nativity of Christ. "Oh, it's just a Christmas custom!" they would have said. A serious answer would require a far-reaching dissertation on the symbolism of the dying god in antiquity, in the Near East, and its relation to the cult of the Great Mother and her symbol, the tree—to mention only one aspect of this complicated problem.

551    The further we delve into the origins of a *représentation collective* or, in ecclesiastical language, of a dogma, the more we uncover a seemingly limitless web of archetypal patterns that, before modern times, were never the object of conscious reflection. Thus, paradoxically enough, we know more about mythological symbolism than did any age before our own. The fact is that in former times men *lived* their symbols rather than reflected upon them. I will illustrate this by an experience I once had with the primitives on Mount Elgon in East Africa. Every morning at dawn they leave their huts and breathe or spit into their hands, stretching them out to the first rays of the sun, as if they were offering either their breath or their spittle to the rising god—to *mungu*. (This Swahili word, which they used in explaining the ritual act, is derived from a Polynesian root equivalent to *mana* or *mulungu*. These and similar terms designate a "power" of extraordinary efficacy, an all-pervading essence which we would call divine. Thus the word *mungu* is their equivalent for Allah or God.) When I asked them what they meant by this act and why they did it, they were completely baffled. They could only say: "We have always done it. It has always been done when the sun rises." They laughed at the obvious conclusion that the sun is *mungu*. The sun is not *mungu* when it is above the horizon; *mungu* is the actual moment of the sunrise.

552    What they were doing was obvious to me but not to them. They just do it, they never reflect on what they are doing, and are consequently unable to explain themselves. They are evidently just repeating what they have "always" done at sunrise, no doubt with a certain emotion and by no means merely mechanically, for they *live* it while we *reflect* on it. Thus I knew that they were offering their *souls* to *mungu*, because the breath (of life) and the spittle mean "soul substance." Breathing or spitting on something conveys a "magical" effect, as, for instance, when Christ used spittle to heal the blind, or when a son inhales his dying father's last breath in order to take over the father's soul. It is most unlikely that these primitives ever, even in the remote past, knew any more about the meaning of their ceremony. On the contrary, their ancestors probably knew even less, because they were more profoundly unconscious and thought if possible even less about their doings.

553   Faust aptly says: "Im Anfang war die Tat" (in the beginning was the deed). Deeds were never invented, they were done. Thoughts, on the other hand, are a relatively late discovery; they were found, and then they were sought and found. Yet unreflected life existed long before man; it was not invented, but in it man found himself as an afterthought. First he was moved to deeds by unconscious factors, and only a long time afterwards did he begin to reflect about the causes that had moved him; then it took him a very long time indeed to arrive at the preposterous idea that he must have moved himself—his mind being unable to see any other motivating force than his own. We would laugh at the idea of a plant or an animal inventing itself, yet there are many people who believe that the psyche or the mind invented itself and thus brought itself into being. As a matter of fact, the mind has grown to its present state of consciousness as an acorn grows into an oak or as saurians developed into mammals. As it has been, so it is still, and thus we are moved by forces from within as well as from without.

554   In a mythological age these forces were called *mana*, spirits, demons, and gods, and they are as active today as they ever were. If they conform to our wishes, we call them happy hunches or impulses and pat ourselves on the back for being smart fellows. If they go against us, then we say it is just bad luck, or that certain people have it in for us, or it must be pathological. The one thing we refuse to admit is that we are dependent on "powers" beyond our control.

555   It is true that civilized man has acquired a certain amount of will-power which he can apply where he pleases. We have learnt to do our work efficiently without having recourse to chanting and drumming to hypnotize us into the state of doing. We can even dispense with the daily prayer for divine aid. We can carry out what we propose to do, and it seems self-evident that an idea can be translated into action without a hitch, whereas the primitive is hampered at every step by doubts, fears, and superstitions. The motto "Where there's a will there's a way" is not just a Germanic prejudice; it is the superstition of modern man in general. In order to maintain his credo, he cultivates a remarkable lack of introspection. He is blind to the fact that, with all his rationality and efficiency, he is possessed by powers beyond his control. The gods and demons have not disappeared at all, they

have merely got new names. They keep him on the run with restlessness, vague apprehensions, psychological complications, an invincible need for pills, alcohol, tobacco, dietary and other hygienic systems—and above, all, with an impressive array of neuroses.

556    I once met a drastic example of this in a professor of philosophy and "psychology"—a psychology in which the unconscious had not yet arrived. He was the man I mentioned who was obsessed by the idea that he had cancer,⁻although X-rays had proved to him that it was all imaginary. Who or what caused this idea? It obviously derived from a fear that was not caused by observation of the facts. It suddenly overcame him and then remained. Symptoms of this kind are extraordinarily obstinate and often enough hinder the patient from getting the proper treatment. For what good would psychotherapy be in dealing with a malignant tumour? Such a dangerous thing could only be operated on without delay. To the professor's ever-renewed relief, every new authority assured him that there was no trace of cancer. But the very next day the doubt began nagging again, and he was plunged once more into the night of unmitigated fear.

557    The morbid thought had a power of its own that he could not control. It was not foreseen in his philosophical brand of psychology, where everything flowed neatly from consciousness and sense-perception. The professor admitted that his case was pathological, but there his thinking stopped, because it had arrived at the sacrosanct border-line between the philosophical and the medical faculty. The one deals with normal and the other with abnormal contents, unknown in the philosopher's world.

558    This compartment psychology reminds me of another case. It was that of an alcoholic who had come under the laudable influence of a certain religious movement and, fascinated by its enthusiasm, had forgotten he needed a drink. He was obviously and miraculously cured by Jesus, and accordingly was held up as a witness to divine grace or to the efficacy of the said organization. After a few weeks of public confession, the novelty began to wear off and some alcoholic refreshment seemed to be indicated. But this time the helpful organization came to the conclusion that the case was "pathological" and not suitable for an

intervention by Jesus. So they put him in a clinic to let the doctor do better than the divine healer.

559     This is an aspect of the modern "cultural" mind that is well worth looking into. It shows an alarming degree of dissociation and psychological confusion. We believe exclusively in consciousness and free will, and are no longer aware of the powers that control us to an indefinite degree, outside the narrow domain where we can be reasonable and exercise a certain amount of free choice and self-control. In our time of general disorientation, it is necessary to know about the true state of human affairs, which depends so much on the mental and moral qualities of the individual and on the human psyche in general. But if we are to see things in their right perspective, we need to understand the past of man as well as his present. That is why a correct understanding of myths and symbols is of essential importance.

## 6. THE FUNCTION OF RELIGIOUS SYMBOLS

560    Although our civilized consciousness has separated itself from the instincts, the instincts have not disappeared; they have merely lost their contact with consciousness. They are thus forced to assert themselves in an indirect way, through what Janet called automatisms. These take the form of symptoms in the case of a neurosis or, in normal cases, of incidents of various kinds, like unaccountable moods, unexpected forgetfulness, mistakes in speech, and so on. Such manifestations show very clearly the *autonomy* of the archetypes. It is easy to believe that one is master in one's own house, but, as long as we are unable to control our emotions and moods, or to be conscious of the myriad secret ways in which unconscious factors insinuate themselves into our arrangements and decisions, we are certainly not the masters. On the contrary, we have so much reason for uncertainty that it will be better to look twice at what we are doing.

561    The exploration of one's conscience, however, is not a popular pastime, although it would be most necessary, particularly in our time when man is threatened with self-created and deadly dangers that are growing beyond his control. If, for a moment, we look at mankind as one individual, we see that it is like a man carried away by unconscious powers. He is dissociated like a neurotic, with the Iron Curtain marking the line of division. Western man, representing the kind of consciousness hitherto regarded as valid, has become increasingly aware of the aggressive will to power of the East, and he sees himself forced to take extraordinary measures of defence. What he fails to see is that it is his own vices, publicly repudiated and covered up by good international manners, that are thrown back in his face through their shameless and methodical application by the East. What the West has tolerated, but only secretly, and indulged in a bit shamefacedly (the diplomatic lie, the double-cross, veiled

threats), comes back openly and in full measure and gets us tied up in knots—exactly the case of the neurotic! It is the face of our own shadow that glowers at us across the Iron Curtain.

562     This state of affairs explains the peculiar feeling of helplessness that is creeping over our Western consciousness. We are beginning to realize that the conflict is in reality a moral and mental problem, and we are trying to find some answer to it. We grow increasingly aware that the nuclear deterrent is a desperate and undesirable answer, as it cuts both ways. We know that moral and mental remedies would be more effective because they could provide us with a psychic immunity to the ever-increasing infection. But all our attempts have proved to be singularly ineffectual, and will continue to do so as long as we try to convince ourselves and the world that it is only *they*, our opponents, who are all wrong, morally and philosophically. We expect *them* to see and understand where they are wrong, instead of making a serious effort ourselves to recognize our own shadow and its nefarious doings. If we could only see our shadow, we should be immune to any moral and mental infection and insinuation. But as long as this is not so, we lay ourselves open to every infection because we are doing practically the same things as *they* are, only with the additional disadvantage that we neither see nor want to understand what we are doing under the cloak of good manners.

563     The East has one big myth—which we call an illusion in the vain hope that our superior judgment will make it disappear. This myth is the time-hallowed archetypal dream of a Golden Age or a paradise on earth, where everything is provided for everybody, and one great, just, and wise Chief rules over a human kindergarten. This powerful archetype in its infantile form has got them all right, but it won't disappear from the world at the mere sight of our superior point of view. We even support it by our own childishness, for our Western civilization is in the grip of the same mythology. We cherish the same prejudices, hopes, and expectations. We believe in the Welfare State, in universal peace, in more or less equality for man, in his eternal human rights, in justice and truth, and (not too loud) in the Kingdom of God on earth.

564     The sad truth is that man's real life consists of inexorable opposites—day and night, wellbeing and suffering, birth and

death, good and evil. We are not even sure that the one will prevail against the other, that good will overcome evil, or joy defeat pain. Life and the world are a battleground, have always been and always will be, and, if it were not so, existence would soon come to an end. It is for this reason that a superior religion like Christianity expected an early end to this world, and Buddhism actually puts an end to it by turning its back on all desires. These categorical answers would be frankly suicidal if they were not bound up with the peculiar moral ideas and practices that constitute the body of both religions.

565     I mention this because in our time there are countless people who have lost faith in one or other of the world religions. They do not understand them any longer. While life runs smoothly, the loss remains as good as unnoticed. But when suffering comes, things change very rapidly. One seeks the way out and begins to reflect about the meaning of life and its bewildering experiences. It is significant that, according to the statistics, the psychiatrist is consulted more by Protestants and Jews than by Catholics. This might be expected, for the Catholic Church still feels responsible for the *cura animarum*, the care of souls. But in this scientific age, the psychiatrist is apt to be asked questions that once belonged to the domain of the theologian. People feel that it makes, or would make, a great difference if only they had a positive belief in a meaningful way of life or in God and immortality. The spectre of death looming up before them often gives a powerful incentive to such thoughts. From time immemorial, men have had ideas about a Supreme Being (one or several) and about the Land of the Hereafter. Only modern man thinks he can do without them. Because he cannot discover God's throne in heaven with a telescope or radar, or establish for certain that dear father or mother are still about in a more or less corporeal form, he assumes that such ideas are not "true." I would rather say that they are not "true" enough. They have accompanied human life since prehistoric times and are still ready to break through into consciousness at the slightest provocation.

566     One even regrets the loss of such convictions. Since it is a matter of invisible and unknowable things (God is beyond human understanding, and immortality cannot be proved), why should we bother about evidence or truth? Suppose we did not

126

know and understand the need for salt in our food, we would nevertheless profit from its use. Even if we should assume that salt is an illusion of our taste-buds, or a superstition, it would still contribute to our wellbeing. Why, then, should we deprive ourselves of views that prove helpful in crises and give a meaning to our existence? And how do we know that such ideas are not true? Many people would agree with me if I stated flatly that such ideas are illusions. What they fail to realize is that this denial amounts to a "belief" and is just as impossible to prove as a religious assertion. We are entirely free to choose our standpoint; it will in any case be an arbitrary decision. There is, however, a strong empirical reason why we should hold beliefs that we know can never be proved. It is that they are known to be useful. Man positively needs general ideas and convictions that will give a meaning to his life and enable him to find his place in the universe. He can stand the most incredible hardships when he is convinced that they make sense; but he is crushed when, on top of all his misfortunes, he has to admit that he is taking part in a "tale told by an idiot."

567     It is the purpose and endeavour of religious symbols to give a meaning to the life of man. The Pueblo Indians believe that they are the sons of Father Sun, and this belief gives their life a perspective and a goal beyond their individual and limited existence. It leaves ample room for the unfolding of their personality, and is infinitely more satisfactory than the certainty that one is and will remain the underdog in a department store. If St. Paul had been convinced that he was nothing but a wandering weaver of carpets, he would certainly not have been himself. His real and meaningful life lay in the certainty that he was the messenger of the Lord. You can accuse him of megalomania, but your opinion pales before the testimony of history and the *consensus omnium*. The myth that took possession of him made him something greater than a mere craftsman.

568     Myths, however, consist of symbols that were not invented but happened. It was not the man Jesus who created the myth of the God-man; it had existed many centuries before. He himself was seized by this symbolic idea, which, as St. Mark tells us, lifted him out of the carpenter's shop and the mental narrowness of his surroundings. Myths go back to primitive story-tellers and their dreams, to men moved by the stirrings of their fanta-

sies, who were not very different from poets and philosophers in later times. Primitive story-tellers never worried about the origin of their fantasies; it was only much later that people began to wonder where the story came from. Already in ancient Greece they were advanced enough to surmise that the stories about the gods were nothing but old and exaggerated traditions of ancient kings and their deeds. They assumed even then that the myth did not mean what it said because it was obviously improbable. Therefore they tried to reduce it to a generally understandable yarn. This is exactly what our time has tried to do with dream symbolism: it is assumed that it does not mean what it seems to say, but something that is generally known and understood, though not openly admitted because of its inferior quality. For those who had got rid of their conventional blinkers there were no longer any riddles. It seemed certain that dreams meant something different from what they said.

569     This assumption is wholly arbitrary. The Talmud says more aptly: "The dream is its own interpretation." Why should dreams mean something different from what appears in them? Is there anything in nature that is other than what it is? For instance, the duck-billed platypus, that original monster which no zoologist would ever have invented, is it not just what it is? The dream is a normal and natural phenomenon, which is certainly just what it is and does not mean something it is not. We call its contents symbolic because they have obviously not only one meaning, but point in different directions and must therefore mean something that is unconscious, or at least not conscious in all its aspects.

570     To the scientific mind, such phenomena as symbolic ideas are most irritating, because they cannot be formulated in a way that satisfies our intellect and logic. They are by no means the only instance of this in psychology. The trouble begins already with the phenomenon of affect or emotion, which evades all the attempts of the psychologist to pin it down in a hard-and-fast concept. The cause of the difficulty is the same in both cases—the intervention of the unconscious. I know enough of the scientific standpoint to understand that it is most annoying to have to deal with facts that cannot be grasped completely or at any rate adequately. The trouble with both phenomena is that the facts are undeniable and yet cannot be formulated in intellectual terms.

Instead of observable détails with clearly discernible features, it is life itself that wells up in emotions and symbolic ideas. In many cases emotion and symbol are actually one and the same thing. There is no intellectual formula capable of representing such a complex phenomenon in a satisfactory way.

571   The academic psychologist is perfectly free to dismiss the emotions or the unconscious, or both, from his consideration. Yet they remain facts to which at least the medical psychologist has to pay ample attention, for emotional conflicts and the interventions of the unconscious are the classical features of his science. If he treats a patient at all, he is confronted with irrationalities of this kind whether he can formulate them intellectually or not. He has to acknowledge their only too troublesome existence. It is therefore quite natural that people who have not had the medical psychologist's experience find it difficult to follow what he is talking about. Anyone who has not had the chance, or the misfortune, to live through the same or similar experiences is hardly capable of understanding what happens when psychology ceases to be a tranquil pursuit for the scientist in his laboratory and becomes a real life adventure. Target practice on a shooting range is far from being a battlefield, but the doctor has to deal with casualties in a real war. Therefore he has to concern himself with psychic realities even if he cannot define them in scientific terms. He can name them, but he knows that all the terms he uses to designate the essentials of life do not pretend to be more than names for facts that have to be experienced in themselves, because they cannot be reproduced by their names. No textbook can teach psychology; one learns only by actual experience. No understanding is gained by memorizing words, for symbols are the living facts of life.

572   The cross in the Christian religion, for instance, is a meaningful symbol that expresses a multitude of aspects, ideas, and emotions, but a cross before somebody's name simply indicates that that individual is dead. The *lingam* or phallus functions as an all-embracing symbol in the Hindu religion, but if a street urchin draws one on a wall, it just means an interest in his penis. Because infantile and adolescent fantasies often continue far into adult life, many dreams contain unmistakable sexual allusions. It would be absurd to understand them as anything else.

But when a mason speaks of monks and nuns to be laid upon each other, or a locksmith of male and female keys, it would be nonsensical to suppose that he is indulging in glowing adolescent fantasies. He simply means a particular kind of tile or key that has been given a colourful name. But when an educated Hindu talks to you about the *lingam*, you will hear things we Westerners would never connect with the penis. You may even find it most difficult to guess what he actually means by this term, and you will naturally conclude that the lingam *symbolizes* a good many things. It is certainly not an obscene allusion; nor is the cross a mere sign for death but a symbol for a great many other ideas. Much, therefore, depends on the maturity of the dreamer who produces such an image.

573 The interpretation of dreams and symbols requires some intelligence. It cannot be mechanized and crammed into stupid and unimaginative brains. It demands an ever-increasing knowledge of the dreamer's individuality as well as an ever-increasing self-awareness on the part of the interpreter. No experienced worker in this field will deny that there are rules of thumb that can prove helpful, but they must be applied with prudence and intelligence. Not everybody can master the "technique." You may follow all the right rules and the apparently safe path of knowledge and yet you get stuck in the most appalling nonsense, simply by overlooking a seemingly unimportant detail that a better intelligence would not have missed. Even a man with a highly developed intellect can go badly astray because he has never learnt to use his intuition or his feeling, which might be at a regrettably low level of development.

574 The attempt to understand symbols does not only bring you up against the symbol itself, but up against the wholeness of the symbol-producing individual. If one is really up to this challenge, one may meet with success. But as a rule it will be necessary to make a special study of the individual and his or her cultural background. One can learn a lot in this way and so get a chance to fill in the gaps in one's education. I have made it a rule myself to consider every case an entirely new proposition about which I do not even know the ABC. Routine may be and often is practical, and quite useful as long as one skates on the surface, but as soon as one gets in touch with the vital problems,

life itself takes over and even the most brilliant theoretical premises become ineffectual words.

575     This makes the teaching of methods and techniques a major problem. As I have said, the pupil has to acquire a good deal of specialized knowledge. This provides him with the necessary mental tool-shop, but the main thing, the handling of the tools, can be acquired only if the pupil undergoes an analysis that acquaints him with his own conflict. This can be quite a task with some so-called normal but unimaginative individuals. They are just incapable of realizing, for instance, the simple fact that psychic events happen to us spontaneously. Such people prefer to cling to the idea that whatever occurs either is done by themselves or else is pathological and must be cured by pills or injections. They show how close dull normality is to a neurosis, and as a matter of fact such people succumb most easily to psychic epidemics.

576     In all the higher grades of science, imagination and intuition play an increasingly important role over and above intellect and its capacity for application. Even physics, the most rigorous of all the applied sciences, depends to an astonishing degree on intuition, which works by way of the unconscious processes and not by logical deductions, although it is possible to demonstrate afterwards what logical procedure might have led to the same result.

577     Intuition is almost indispensable in the interpretation of symbols, and can cause an immediate acceptance on the part of the dreamer. But, subjectively convincing as such a lucky hunch may be, it is also somewhat dangerous, because it leads to a false sense of security. It may even seduce both the interpreter and the dreamer into continuing this rather facile exchange of ideas, which may end in a sort of mutual dream. The secure basis of real intellectual and moral knowledge gets lost if one is satisfied with a vague feeling of having understood. Usually when one asks people the reasons for their so-called understanding, they are unable to give an explanation. One can understand and explain only when one has brought intuitions down to the safe basis of real knowledge of the facts and their logical connections. An honest investigator will have to admit that this is not possible in certain cases, but it would be dishonest of him to dismiss them on that account. Even a scientist is a human being, and it

is quite natural that he, like others, hates the things he cannot explain and thus falls victim to the common illusion that what we know today represents the highest summit of knowledge. Nothing is more vulnerable and ephemeral than scientific theories, which are mere tools and not everlasting truths.

## 7. HEALING THE SPLIT

578    When the medical psychologist takes an interest in symbols, he is primarily concerned with "natural" symbols as distinct from "cultural" symbols. The former are derived from the unconscious contents of the psyche, and they therefore represent an enormous number of variations on the basic archetypal motifs. In many cases, they can be traced back to their archaic roots, i.e., to ideas and images that we meet in the most ancient records and in primitive societies. In this respect, I should like to call the reader's attention to such books as Mircea Eliade's study of shamanism,[1] where a great many illuminating examples may be found.

579    "Cultural" symbols, on the other hand, are those that have expressed "eternal truths" or are still in use in many religions. They have gone through many transformations and even a process of more or less conscious elaboration, and in this way have become the *représentations collectives* of civilized societies. Nevertheless, they have retained much of their original numinosity, and they function as positive or negative "prejudices" with which the psychologist has to reckon very seriously.

580    Nobody can dismiss these numinous factors on merely rational grounds. They are important constituents of our mental make-up and vital forces in the building up of human society, and they cannot be eradicated without serious loss. When they are repressed or neglected, their specific energy disappears into the unconscious with unpredictable consequences. The energy that appears to have been lost revives and intensifies whatever is uppermost in the unconscious—tendencies, perhaps, that have hitherto had no chance to express themselves, or have not been allowed an uninhibited existence in our consciousness. They

[1] *Shamanism: Archaic Techniques of Ecstasy* (1964).

form an ever-present destructive "shadow." Even tendencies that might be able to exert a beneficial influence turn into veritable demons when they are repressed. This is why many well-meaning people are understandably afraid of the unconscious, and incidentally of psychology.

581 Our times have demonstrated what it means when the gates of the psychic underworld are thrown open. Things whose enormity nobody could have imagined in the idyllic innocence of the first decade of our century have happened and have turned the world upside down. Ever since, the world has remained in a state of schizophrenia. Not only has the great civilized Germany disgorged its primitivity, but Russia also is ruled by it, and Africa has been set on fire. No wonder the Western world feels uneasy, for it does not know how much it plays into the hands of the uproarious underworld and what it has lost through the destruction of its numinosities. It has lost its moral and spiritual values to a very dangerous degree. Its moral and spiritual tradition has collapsed, and has left a worldwide disorientation and dissociation.

582 We could have seen long ago from primitive societies what the loss of numinosity means: they lose their *raison d'être*, the order of their social organizations, and then they dissolve and decay. We are now in the same condition. We have lost something we have never properly understood. Our spiritual leaders cannot be spared the blame for having been more interested in protecting their institutions than in understanding the mystery that symbols present. Faith does not exclude thought (which is man's strongest weapon), but unfortunately many believers are so afraid of science, and also of psychology, that they turn a blind eye to the numinous psychic powers that forever control man's fate. We have stripped all things of their mystery and numinosity; nothing is holy any longer.

583 The masses and their leaders do not realize that it makes no substantial difference whether you call the world principle male and a father (spirit), or female and a mother (matter). Essentially, we know as little of the one as of the other. Since the beginning of the human mind, both were numinous symbols, and their importance lay in their numinosity and not in their sex or other chance attributes. Since energy never vanishes, the emotional energy that manifests itself in all numinous phenom-

ena does not cease to exist when it disappears from consciousness. As I have said, it reappears in unconscious manifestations, in symbolic happenings that compensate the disturbances of the conscious psyche. Our psyche is profoundly disturbed by the loss of moral and spiritual values that have hitherto kept our life in order. Our consciousness is no longer capable of integrating the natural afflux of concomitant, instinctive events that sustains our conscious psychic activity. This process can no longer take place in the same way as before, because our consciousness has deprived itself of the organs by which the auxiliary contributions of the instincts and the unconscious could be assimilated. These organs were the numinous symbols, held holy by common consent.

584    A concept like "physical matter," stripped of its numinous connotation of the "Great Mother," no longer expresses the vast emotional meaning of "Mother Earth." It is a mere intellectual term, dry as dust and entirely inhuman. In the same way, "spirit" identified with "intellect" ceases to be the Father of All. It degenerates into the limited mind of man, and the immense emotional energy expressed in the image "our Father" vanishes in the sand of an intellectual desert.

585    Through scientific understanding, our world has become dehumanized. Man feels himself isolated in the cosmos. He is no longer involved in nature and has lost his emotional participation in natural events, which hitherto had a symbolic meaning for him. Thunder is no longer the voice of a god, nor is lightning his avenging missile. No river contains a spirit, no tree means a man's life, no snake is the embodiment of wisdom, and no mountain still harbours a great demon. Neither do things speak to him nor can he speak to things, like stones, springs, plants, and animals. He no longer has a bush-soul identifying him with a wild animal. His immediate communication with nature is gone for ever, and the emotional energy it generated has sunk into the unconscious.

586    This enormous loss is compensated by the symbols in our dreams. They bring up our original nature, its instincts and its peculiar thinking. Unfortunately, one would say, they also express their contents in the language of nature, which is strange and incomprehensible to us. It sets us the task of translating its images into the rational words and concepts of modern speech,

which has liberated itself from its primitive encumbrances—notably from its mystical participation with things. Nowadays, talking of ghosts and other numinous figures is no longer the same as conjuring them up. We have ceased to believe in magical formulas; not many taboos and similar restrictions are left; and our world seems to be disinfected of all such superstitious numina as "witches, warlocks, and worricows," to say nothing of werewolves, vampires, bush-souls, and all the other bizarre beings that populate the primeval forest.

587 At least the surface of our world seems to be purified of all superstitious and irrational admixtures. Whether, however, the real inner world of man—and not our wish-fulfilling fiction about it—is also freed from primitivity is another question. Is not the number 13 still taboo for many people? Are there not still many individuals possessed by funny prejudices, projections, and illusions? A realistic picture of the human mind reveals many primitive traits and survivals, which are still playing their roles just as if nothing had happened during the last five hundred years. The man of today is a curious mixture of characteristics acquired over the long ages of his mental development. This is the man and his symbols we have to deal with, and we must scrutinize his mental products very carefully indeed. Sceptical viewpoints and scientific convictions exist in him side by side with old-fashioned prejudices, outdated habits of thought and feeling, obstinate misinterpretations, and blind ignorance.

588 Such are the people who produce the symbols we are investigating in their dreams. In order to explain the symbols and their meaning, it is essential to learn whether these representations are still the same as they ever were, or whether they have been chosen by the dream for its particular purpose from a store of general conscious knowledge. If, for instance, one has to deal with a dream in which the number 13 occurs, the question is: Does the dreamer habitually believe in the unfavourable nature of the number, or does the dream merely allude to people who still indulge in such superstitions? The answer will make a great difference to the interpretation. In the former case, the dreamer is still under the spell of the unlucky 13, and will therefore feel most uncomfortable in room no. 13 or sitting at a table with thirteen people. In the latter case, 13 may not be more than a chiding or disparaging remark. In one case it is a still numinous

representation; in the other it is stripped of its original emotionality and has assumed the innocuous character of a mere piece of indifferent information.

589    This illustrates the way in which archetypes appear in practical experience. In the first case they appear in their original form—they are images and at the same time emotions. One can speak of an archetype only when these two aspects coincide. When there is only an image, it is merely a word-picture, like a corpuscle with no electric charge. It is then of little consequence, just a word and nothing more. But if the image is charged with numinosity, that is, with psychic energy, then it becomes dynamic and will produce consequences. It is a great mistake in practice to treat an archetype as if it were a mere name, word, or concept. It is far more than that: it is a piece of life, an image connected with the living individual by the bridge of emotion. The word alone is a mere abstraction, an exchangeable coin in intellectual commerce. But the archetype is living matter. It is not limitlessly exchangeable but always belongs to the economy of a living individual, from which it cannot be detached and used arbitrarily for different ends. It cannot be explained in just any way, but only in the one that is indicated by that particular individual. Thus the symbol of the cross, in the case of a good Christian, can be interpreted only in the Christian way unless the dream produces very strong reasons to the contrary, and even then the specifically Christian meaning should not be lost sight of.

590    The mere use of words is futile if you do not know what they stand for. This is particularly true in psychology, where we speak of archetypes like the anima and animus, the wise old man, the great mother, and so on. You can know about all the saints, sages, prophets, and other godly men, and all the great mothers of the world, but if they are mere images whose numinosity you have never experienced, it will be as if you were talking in a dream, for you do not know what you are talking about. The words you use are empty and valueless, and they gain life and meaning only when you try to learn about their numinosity, their relationship to the living individual. Then only do you begin to understand that the names mean very little, but that the way they are related to you is all-important.

591    The symbol-producing function of our dreams is an attempt

to bring our original mind back to consciousness, where it has never been before, and where it has never undergone critical self-reflection. We *have been* that mind, but we have never *known* it. We got rid of it before understanding it. It rose from its cradle, shedding its primitive characteristics like cumbersome and valueless husks. It looks as if the unconscious represented the deposit of these remnants. Dreams and their symbols continually refer to them, as if they intended to bring back all the old primitive things from which the mind freed itself in the course of its evolution: illusions, childish fantasies, archaic thought-forms, primitive instincts. This is in reality the case, and it explains the resistance, even fear and horror, one experiences in approaching the unconscious. One is shocked less by the primitivity of its contents than by their emotionality. They are not merely neutral or indifferent, they are so charged with affect that they are often exceedingly uncomfortable. They can even cause real panic, and the more they are repressed the more they spread through the whole personality in the form of a neurosis.

592    It is just their emotionality, however, that gives them such a vital importance. It is as if a man who has lived through a period of life in an unconscious state should suddenly realize that there is a gap in his memory—that important events seem to have taken place that he cannot remember. In so far as he assumes that the psyche is an exclusively personal affair (and this is the usual assumption), he will try to retrieve the apparently lost infantile memories. But the gaps in his childhood memories are merely the symptoms of a much greater loss, the loss of the primitive psyche—the psyche that lived and functioned before it was reflected by consciousness.

593    As the evolution of the embryonic body repeats its prehistory, so the mind grows up through the series of its prehistoric stages. Dreams seem to consider it their main task to bring back a sort of recollection of the prehistoric as well as the infantile world, right down to the level of the most primitive instincts, as if such memories were a priceless treasure. And these memories can indeed have a remarkably healing effect in certain cases, as Freud saw long ago. This observation confirms the view that an infantile memory-gap (a so-called amnesia) amounts to a definite loss and that its recovery brings an increase in vitality and well-being. Since we measure a child's psychic life by the

paucity and simplicity of its conscious contents, we do not appreciate the far-reaching complexities of the infantile mind that stem from its original identity with the prehistoric psyche. That "original mind" is just as much present and still functioning in the child as the evolutionary stages are in the embryo. If the reader remembers what I said earlier about the child who made a present of her dreams to her father, he will get a good idea of what I mean.

594    In infantile amnesia, one finds strange admixtures of mythological fragments that also often appear in later psychoses. Images of this kind are highly numinous and therefore very important. If such recollections reappear in adult life, they may in some cases cause profound psychological disturbances, while in other people they can produce astonishing cures or religious conversions. Often they bring back a piece of life, missing for a long time, that enriches the life of an individual.

595    The recollection of infantile memories and the reproduction of archetypal modes of psychic functioning create a wider horizon and a greater extension of consciousness, provided that one succeeds in assimilating and integrating the lost and regained contents. Since they are not neutral, their assimilation will modify the personality, even as they themselves will have to undergo certain alterations. In this part of the individuation process the interpretation of symbols plays an important practical role; for the symbols are natural attempts to reconcile and reunite often widely separated opposites, as is apparent from the contradictory nature of many symbols. It would be a particularly obnoxious error in this work of assimilation if the interpreter were to take only the conscious memories as "true" or "real," while considering the archetypal contents as merely fantastic representations. Dreams and their ambiguous symbols owe their forms on the one hand to repressed contents and on the other to archetypes. They thus have two aspects and enable one to interpret in two ways: one lays the emphasis either on their personal or on their archetypal aspect. The former shows the morbid influence of repression and infantile wishes, while the latter points to the sound instinctive basis. However fantastic the archetypal contents may be, they represent emotional powers or "numinosities." If one should try to brush them aside, they would only get repressed and would create the same neurotic condition as be-

fore. Their numinosity gives the contents an autonomous nature. This is a psychological fact that cannot be denied. If it is nevertheless denied, the regained contents are annihilated and any attempt at a synthesis is futile. But it appears to be a tempting way out and therefore it is often chosen.

596    Not only is the existence of archetypes denied, but even those people who do admit their existence usually treat them as if they were mere images and forget that they are living entities that make up a great part of the human psyche. As soon as the interpreter strips them of their numinosity, they lose their life and become mere words. It is then easy enough to link them together with other mythological representations, and so the process of limitless substitution begins; one glides from archetype to archetype, everything means everything, and one has reduced the whole process to absurdity. All the corpses in the world are chemically identical, but living individuals are not. It is true that the forms of archetypes are to a considerable extent interchangeable, but their numinosity is and remains a fact. It represents the *value* of an archetypal event. This emotional value must be kept in mind and allowed for throughout the whole intellectual process of interpretation. The risk of losing it is great, because thinking and feeling are so diametrically opposed that thinking abolishes feeling-values and vice versa. Psychology is the only science that has to take the factor of value (feeling) into account, since it forms the link between psychic events on the one hand, and meaning and life on the other.

597    Our intellect has created a new world that dominates nature, and has populated it with monstrous machines. The latter are so indubitably useful and so much needed that we cannot see even a possibility of getting rid of them or of our odious subservience to them. Man is bound to follow the exploits of his scientific and inventive mind and to admire himself for his splendid achievements. At the same time, he cannot help admitting that his genius shows an uncanny tendency to invent things that become more and more dangerous, because they represent better and better means for wholesale suicide. In view of the rapidly increasing avalanche of world population, we have already begun to seek ways and means of keeping the rising flood at bay. But nature may anticipate all our attempts by turning against man his own creative mind, and, by releasing the H-bomb or some

equally catastrophic device, put an effective stop to over-
population. In spite of our proud domination of nature we are
still her victims as much as ever and have not even learnt to
control our own nature, which slowly and inevitably courts disaster.

598    There are no longer any gods whom we can invoke to help
us. The great religions of the world suffer from increasing anae-
mia, because the helpful numina have fled from the woods,
rivers, mountains, and animals, and the God-men have disappeared underground into the unconscious. There we suppose
they lead an ignominious existence among the relics of our past,
while we remain dominated by the great *Déesse Raison*, who is
our overwhelming illusion. With her aid we are doing laudable
things: we rid the world of malaria, we spread hygiene everywhere, with the result that under-developed populations increase at such a rate that food is becoming a problem. "We have
conquered nature" is a mere slogan. In reality we are confronted
with anxious questions, the answers to which seem nowhere in
sight. The so-called conquest of nature overwhelms us with the
natural fact of over-population and makes our troubles more or
less unmanageable because of our psychological incapacity to
reach the necessary political agreements. It remains quite natural for men to quarrel and fight and struggle for superiority over
one another. Where indeed have we "conquered nature"?

599    As any change must begin somewhere, it is the single individual who will undergo it and carry it through. The change
must begin with one individual; it might be any one of us. Nobody can afford to look around and to wait for somebody else to
do what he is loath to do himself. As nobody knows what he
could do, he might be bold enough to ask himself whether by
any chance his unconscious might know something helpful,
when there is no satisfactory conscious answer anywhere in sight.
Man today is painfully aware of the fact that neither his great
religions nor his various philosophies seem to provide him with
those powerful ideas that would give him the certainty and security he needs in face of the present condition of the world.

600    I know that the Buddhists would say, as indeed they do: if
only people would follow the noble eightfold path of the
Dharma (doctrine, law) and had true insight into the Self; or
the Christians: if only people had the right faith in the Lord; or

the rationalists: if only people could be intelligent and reasonable—then all problems would be manageable and solvable. The trouble is that none of them manages to solve these problems himself. Christians often ask why God does not speak to them, as he is believed to have done in former days. When I hear such questions, it always makes me think of the Rabbi who was asked how it could be that God often showed himself to people in the olden days but that nowadays one no longer saw him. The Rabbi replied: "Nor is there anyone nowadays who could stoop so low."

601 This answer hits the nail on the head. We are so captivated by and entangled in our subjective consciousness that we have simply forgotten the age-old fact that God speaks chiefly through dreams and visions. The Buddhist discards the world of unconscious fantasies as "distractions" and useless illusions; the Christian puts his Church and his Bible between himself and his unconscious; and the rationalist intellectual does not yet know that his consciousness is not his total psyche, in spite of the fact that for more than seventy years the unconscious has been a basic scientific concept that is indispensable to any serious student of psychology.

602 We can no longer afford to be so God-almighty as to set ourselves up as judges of the merits or demerits of natural phenomena. We do not base our botany on a division into useful and useless plants, or our zoology on a classification into harmless and dangerous animals. But we still go on blithely assuming that consciousness is sense and the unconscious is nonsense—as if you could make out whether any natural phenomenon makes sense or not! Do microbes, for instance, make sense or nonsense? Such evaluations merely demonstrate the lamentable state of our mind, which conceals its ignorance and incompetence under the cloak of megalomania. Certainly microbes are very small and most despicable, but it would be folly to know nothing about them.

603 Whatever else the unconscious may be, it is a natural phenomenon that produces symbols, and these symbols prove to be meaningful. We cannot expect someone who has never looked through a microscope to be an authority on microbes; in the same way, no one who has not made a serious study of natural symbols can be considered a competent judge in this matter. But

the general undervaluation of the human psyche is so great that neither the great religions nor the philosophies nor scientific rationalism have been willing to look at it twice. In spite of the fact that the Catholic Church admits the occurrence of dreams sent by God, most of its thinkers make no attempt to understand them. I also doubt whether there is a Protestant treatise on dogmatics that would "stoop so low" as to consider the possibility that the *vox Dei* might be perceived in a dream. But if somebody really believes in God, by what authority does he suggest that God is unable to speak through dreams?

604    I have spent more than half a century investigating natural symbols, and I have come to the conclusion that dreams and their symbols are not stupid and meaningless. On the contrary, dreams provide you with the most interesting information if only you take the trouble to understand their symbols. The results, it is true, have little to do with such worldly concerns as buying and selling. But the meaning of life is not exhaustively explained by your business activities, nor is the deep desire of the human heart answered by your bank account, even if you have never heard of anything else.

605    At a time when all available energy is spent in the investigation of nature, very little attention is paid to the essence of man, which is his psyche, although many researches are made into its conscious functions. But the really unknown part, which produces symbols, is still virtually unexplored. We receive signals from it every night, yet deciphering these communications seems to be such an odious task that very few people in the whole civilized world can be bothered with it. Man's greatest instrument, his psyche, is little thought of, if not actually mistrusted and despised. "It's only psychological" too often means: It is nothing.

606    Where, exactly, does this immense prejudice come from? We have obviously been so busy with the question of what *we* think that we entirely forget what the unconscious psyche thinks about us. Freud made a serious attempt to show why the unconscious deserves no better judgment, and his teachings have inadvertently increased and confirmed the existing contempt for the psyche. Before him it had been merely overlooked and neglected; now it has become a dump for moral refuse and a source of fear.

607     This modern standpoint is surely onesided and unjust. It does not even accord with the known facts. Our actual knowledge of the unconscious shows it to be a natural phenomenon, and that, like nature herself, it is at least *neutral*. It contains all aspects of human nature—light and dark, beautiful and ugly, good and evil, profound and silly. The study of individual as well as collective symbolism is an enormous task, and one that has not yet been mastered. But at last a beginning has been made. The results so far gained are encouraging, and they seem to indicate an answer to many of the questions perplexing present-day mankind.

# PRINCETON/BOLLINGEN PAPERBACK EDITIONS

## FROM THE COLLECTED WORKS OF C. G. JUNG

Aion (96)
Alchemical Studies (13)
Archetypes and the Collective Unconscious (9a)
The Development of Personality (17)
Mysterium Coniunctionis (14)
The Practice of Psychotherapy (16)
Psychological Types (6)
Psychology and Alchemy (12)
Spirit in Man, Art, and Literature (15)
Symbols of Transformation (5)
Two Essays on Analytical Psychology (7)

## TOPICAL SELECTIONS FROM THE COLLECTED WORKS

Answer to Job
Aspects of the Feminine
Aspects of the Masculine
Dreams
Flying Saucers
Four Archetypes
On the Nature of the Psyche
Psychology and the East
Psychology and the Occult
Psychology and Western Religion
Synchronicity
The Undiscovered Self

## ENCOUNTERING JUNG SERIES

Jung on Active Imagination
Jung on Alchemy

Jung on Christianity
Jung on Death and Immortality
Jung on Evil
Jung on Mythology

## ANTHOLOGIES, LETTERS, AND STUDIES

The Basic Writings of C. G. Jung
C. G. Jung Speaking
The Essential Jung
The Freud/Jung Letters (abridged edition)
The Gnostic Jung
Psyche and Symbol
Psychological Reflections

## SEMINARS

Analytical Psychology: Notes of the Seminar Given in 1925
Children's Dreams: Notes from the Seminar Given in 1936–1940
Nietzsche's *Zarathustra*: Notes of the Seminar Given in 1934–1939
The Psychology of Kundalini Yoga: Notes of the Seminar Given in 1932